I0213121

# Whereof:

## poems after Wittgenstein

### Christopher Norris

The right of Christopher Norris to be identified as the author of this work has been asserted by him in accordance with the Copyright, Designs and Patents Act, 1988.

Copyright ©2025 Christopher Norris.

ISBN 978-1-9192698-2-5

All rights reserved. No part of this publication may be reproduced, stored in retrieval system or transmitted in any form or by any means electronic, mechanical, photocopying, recording or otherwise, without the prior permission of the publisher, except in the case of brief quotations embodied in critical articles and reviews.

Published by
Llyfrau Cambria Books, Wales, United Kingdom.
Cambria Books and Cambria Stories are imprints of
Cambria Publishing Ltd.
Discover our other books at: www.cambriabooks.co.uk

*Whereof one cannot speak, thereof one should remain silent.*

Ludwig Wittgenstein

# Dedication

To Stephen and Christine

# Acknowledgments

For many and varied reasons I should especially like to thank Gary Day, Freda Edis, Edward Greenwood, Rahim and Wendy Hassan, Bill Hughes, Rebekah Humphreys, Jennifer Johnson, Peter Thabit Jones, Kathleen Kerr-Koch, Jean Morris, Lucy Newlyn, Nithin Varghese, and Paul Webb. My wife Valerie was unfailingly supportive and put up with many patches of unsociable brooding on my part. As a writer who has published five novels with Cambria she joins me in thanking Chris Jones for his splendid initiative and constant encouragement.

Swansea     October 2025

# CONTENTS

# Foreword

This is a collection of poems and verse-essays about the Austrian-born though British-domiciled philosopher Ludwig Wittgenstein (1889-1951). He is among the best-known and most influential thinkers of the twentieth century, a status not unchallenged but still pretty much accepted in Anglophone quarters. The influence has been mainly on developments in areas such as philosophy of language, ethics, aesthetics, religion, history, and – less centrally – epistemology, metaphysics, and science. One effect of Wittgenstein's overriding concern with language in its various social, cultural, and communicative aspects is the way that those other disciplines have tended to take a markedly 'linguistic turn' over the past seven decades or so, a turn that has come about partly through his having made it so crucial to his thinking. To his later thinking, I should add, since Wittgenstein's work falls roughly into two categories where the 'early' period (epitomised by his *Tractatus Logico-Philosophicus*, pub. 1922) has more to do with formal logic and truth-functions than natural language, while the later phase (most typically the *Philosophical Investigations*, pub. 1953) very pointedly reverses that order of priority. The *Tractatus* was the only book of his that appeared during his lifetime though since then there has been a veritable industry of posthumous texts compiled and edited by his first-generation students and their successors.

I shall not say very much more by way of introduction since my poems aim to provide readers who don't know very much about Wittgenstein with enough information about life and works to make him a less forbidding figure. There are also epigraphs – one or more for each poem – which are taken from various of his works and placed up front to give some basic idea of what's going on. I should say that I regard Wittgenstein as a fascinating writer, and one who in a sense lived up to his own suggestion that '[p]hilosophy ought really to be written only as a form of poetry'. There is certainly something poetic – suggestive, haunting, resonant, moving, evocative, cryptic, or profound – about many of his remarks, among them some that have passed beyond academe to the wider sphere of cultural discourse. However, what Wittgenstein had in mind as 'poetry', in principle and practice, was not at all the kind of verse-commentary or verse-reflection that the reader will encounter here. His implied reference-point for the above remark was poetry in the German early-nineteenth to early twentieth-century line of descent – prototypically Hölderlin and Rilke – where image, metaphor and symbol are strongly foregrounded while discursive reasoning, though sometimes present, tends to be less prominent, as does the supposedly 'prosaic' trope of metonymy. Again, my poems almost systematically invert those priorities. Generically speaking, they are verse-essays and address aspects of Wittgenstein's thought – as succinctly represented by the epigraphs – across a range of discursive, narrative, expository, interpretative, and sometimes psychoanalytic registers. They distance themselves from more familiar ideas of 'the poetic' in order to engage more closely with just that prevalent receptive ethos. Indeed, I intend this sequence as a contribution to philosophical debate around Wittgenstein's thought, albeit a somewhat left-field or heterodox contribution, and one to which verse – with its distinctive prosodic and formal features – is integral at every point.

In a similar vein, I should make it clear that I have written a good deal about Wittgenstein over four decades while wearing my academic-philosopher's hat. Moreover, much of what I have written is substantially at odds with various things he has to say, or – just as often – ways that the commentariat would have him say or intend them. The disagreements focus chiefly on the later work and his version of the 'linguistic turn' which, in condensed but not overly tendentious summary, treats 'language-games' and their associated cultural 'forms of life' as setting the terms for every human activity, discipline, or field of enquiry. That is, they take us as far as we can reasonably hope to go in making good our knowledge or our justificatory grounds for some given truth-claim. At this point, he says, 'I have reached bedrock', since 'then I am inclined to say: this is simply what I do'. But 'what I do' becomes, for Wittgenstein and his followers, 'how some communally accepted and practised language-game allows or requires me to describe and interpret what I do'. And this has now given rise to a school of thought for which language indeed goes 'all the way down', so that any claim for the existence of objective or language/knowledge-independent truths or realities can only be the product of a deeply deluded 'metaphysical' worldview. I think Wittgenstein is wrong about this and that such errors have done great harm not only to academic philosophy – which they often seem on the point of collapsing into one or other of the social sciences – but to human life and culture more broadly. At worst, they have provided pseudo-philosophical cover for 'post-truth' and other such facile notions whose glibly *au courant* usage has enabled some politically disastrous developments in the US and elsewhere.

These pieces are therefore not intended as outright celebrations or poetically inflected endorsements of Wittgenstein's philosophical thought. Rather, they are reckonings with aspects of it which I felt could be revealed – and sometimes contested – in a sequence of rhymed and metrical verse-essays alive to what's distinctively poetic (in a non-received sense) about his characteristic modes of expression. Rhyme and meter are essential to this exercise in so far as they embody poetry's claim to have its own specific angle – or *point d'appui* – on what's left unexamined, or not fully brought out, in prose discourse. Rhyme is a speculative instrument that takes the rhymer from some given launch-point – most often, here, a word or detail in the epigraph – to regions of thought that are often, especially with complex and extended rhyme-schemes, strikingly far-removed from that point. Meter sets up an alternating pattern of convergence with and divergence from natural speech-rhythms and thus goes to emphasise certain salient emphases, doubts, or qualifications. And in the counterpoint of syntax and prosody – or what prose discourse normally requires and what verse imposes through prosodic features like enjambement, stanza-form, or metrical beat – verse can function as a critical check on what prose (including Wittgenstein's 'poetic' prose) must leave unsaid through its own less conspicuous formal demands. My purpose is to put the case for verse as a means of holding Wittgensteinian prose-poetry to standards very different from those that pertain if one simply accepts his remark about philosophizing in or through poetry.

The secondary literature contains a good deal of biographical, anecdotal, and speculative – often psycho-investigative – debate concerning the relationship between Wittgenstein's life and work. This includes discussion of his clearly autistic psychological traits, his obsessional behaviour, his sexual preferences, his fears of madness, and related topics whose bearing on his philosophy is challenged by some, among them – unsurprisingly – those of his students and colleagues for whom he stands as the epitome of 'pure' philosophical intellect. Such topics figure intermittently here as a kind of running subtext where one advantage of verse, as compared with prose exposition, is the way that rhyme and other prosodic devices allow the setting up of associative, metaphorical, or analogical links between very different levels of engagement. For instance, it serves to make the point more effectively that there is a curious – and thought-provoking – tension between Wittgenstein's intense desire for privacy and his insistence on the flat impossibility of conceiving anything like a 'private language' cut off from communal discourses, language-games, or cultural life-forms. Indeed, that point could be broadened to suggest that ultra-subjective or 'confessional' poetry of the type lately prominent among Anglophone writers is itself an instance of diminishing returns for just such Wittgensteinian reasons.

Readers might like to jump forward to Poem 29, 'Trying to say the whole thing', where the epigraph connects that recurrent and achingly frustrated desire with the acute loneliness that comes over thinkers – call them intellectuals – who feel themselves forced into social isolation by the complexity of their thoughts and feelings. The poem involves a curious three-way crossing of communicative paths between Wittgenstein, the brilliant critic-poet William Empson, and the formidable literary critic F.R. Leavis, all of them Cambridge-based at the time (early 1930s) and the topic of shared interest being Empson's riddling yet cosmically expansive early poem 'Legal Fictions'. As a long-time devoted Empsonian I am more often struck by the contrasts than the resemblances between him and Wittgenstein. However, one trait they do have in common is that sense of the chronic isolation experienced by 'complex' individuals who frequently – as many people noted of Wittgenstein – feel a longing for the company of 'simple' (not stupid or necessarily uneducated but intellectually and emotionally straightforward) persons. Empson's extraordinary book *Some Versions of Pastoral* (1935) actually made 'putting the complex into the simple' his elusive generic *fil conducteur* through texts from Elizabethan literature to *Alice in Wonderland*. Of the latter he remarks:

> Once at least in each book a cry of loneliness goes up from Alice at the oddity beyond sympathy or communication of the world she has entered – whether that in which the child is shut by weakness, or the adult by the renunciations necessary both for the ideal and the worldly way of life (the strength of the snobbery is to imply that these are the same).

Snobbery was nowhere in Wittgenstein's psychological make-up, despite his membership of one of the wealthiest families in Austria (he gave away most of his inheritance and far preferred working-class company). His late-life hankering to escape the elitist intellectual buzz-saws of Cambridge and revisit Swansea was evidence enough of genuine, not cultivated, feelings in this regard. He got on well with children for the most part and would likely have appreciated Empson's notion of the child Alice somehow containing in herself – or her habits of thought – all the above-cited complications.

There are many such signs of a strong temperamental if not, in most respects, intellectual or philosophical kinship between Empson and Wittgenstein. Empson's last published poem, 'Let It Go', brings it out very clearly:

It is this deep blankness is the real thing strange.
The more things happen to you, the more you can't
Tell or remember even what they were.

The contradictions cover such a range.
The talk would talk and go so far aslant.
You don't want madhouse and the whole thing there.

Turn again to Poem 29 – 'Trying to say the whole thing' – and the echoes of Wittgenstein become ignorable, along with the fear of madness (see Poem 37) and the 'contradictions', such a prominent theme throughout Empson's life and work. The great difference is that Empson remained a scientifically clued-up critic-poet and a sturdily rationalist believer in the power of, as well as the urgent need for, human reason to do its proper work. Where Wittgenstein in the end pretty much gave up on Russell for sharing precisely those proclivities, Empson always admired him as a defender of progressive, liberal, secular-humanist values. Poem 20 – 'Where Frazer got it wrong?' – will give some idea of how far Wittgenstein went in his rearguard defence of 'magical' thinking and his later outlook of resolute anti-scientism.

So much for what I am attempting here in broadly poetic and philosophical terms. The collection starts with five short poems of a fairly irreverent kind intended to set the tone and exemplify some of the points made above concerning matters of verse-technique and the relation of 'life' to 'work'. After that, they tend to increase in length as the treatment goes deeper or becomes more complex and the reader – I would hope – gains in confidence and grasp. I have therefore organised the sequence with a view to aiding that process rather than (say) for thematic continuity or life-time chronology. The epigraphs are drawn from a wide variety of Wittgenstein texts and can be tracked back to source readily enough via Google or other search engines. (This is primarily a book of poetry rather than an academic treatise so I didn't want to overburden the text with scholarly references.) The poems or individual verse-sequences are listed on the Contents page mostly by title, but in a few cases by some distinctive phrase from the epigraph. The aim has always been to help readers, whether seasoned or novice Wittgensteinians, to find their way around. They are all numbered and normally have titles except in cases where these would most naturally coincide with the epigraph so that the latter is all that's needed.

Readers should have no difficulty in telling from personal pronouns and contextual clues which pieces are to be taken as spoken by Wittgenstein, which by the present author (in poet's or philosopher's hat, or both), and which by a third-party collocutor who may take the role of friend, critic, or – on occasion – jovial scold. There are some anachronisms of usage and idiom but none, I hope, too jarring. I use Arabic numerals for individual poems, whether short or long, and Roman numerals for sub-sections within verse-essays where the piece is intended to be read as a whole.

# 1 Fly and Fly-Bottle

*What is your aim in philosophy? To show the fly the way*
*out of the fly-bottle.*

Ah, but the poor flies buzz around it still,
That bottle you contrived, now almost airless;
And they'll no doubt buzz ceaselessly until
Somebody leaves the stopper out – so careless!


# 2 If a lion could talk . . . .

*If a lion could talk, we could not understand him.*

Well yes, but then, to wonder 'Does he talk,
And if so, how interpret that great roar?'
May be less helpful than to run, not walk,
And show what legs, not language-games, are for.


# 3 Whereof one cannot speak . . . .

*Whereof one cannot speak, thereof one must remain silent.*

Sound enough maxim though, one must observe,
In his case it's 'more honoured in the breach',
Since, after all, it took a certain nerve
To constantly not practise what he'd preach.

# 4 Showing and Saying

*What can be shown, cannot be said.*

Out there, beyond the limits of the known,
Who knows what can or can't be shown or said?
One thing's for sure in this, our mortal zone:
Your gift's less food for thought than stones for bread.

# 5 Philosophical Jokes

*A serious and good philosophical work could be written consisting entirely of jokes.*

True no doubt, Ludwig, but one might demur
Should someone say 'why didn't Wittgenstein
Give us a few?', while wiser folk concur:
'Smart-ass one-liners? Really not his line'.

# 6 The limits of my language . . . .

*The limits of my language are the limits of my world.*

Flat-earther to round-earther: 'see my map!
Push words too far, you'll drop right off the edge.
Those language-gamesters should just cut the crap,
Head home, and take the common-usage pledge'.

Round-earther: 'choose projections fit to wrap
Around the Earth; then that risk you allege
Turns out a language-generated trap
In need of some good sense-supplying wedge'.

But, either way, there's Ludwig keen to tell
Cartographers: 'it's language-games decide
World-boundaries, horizons, and where dwell
The dragons loosed when words are misapplied'.

So harken to him if you'd lift the spell
Of errant language-games or misapplied
Locutions that his word alone can quell –
And thus keep those flat-earthers well onside!

# 7 A Letter to Paul Engelmann

*I once wanted to give a few words in the foreword which
now actually are not in it, which, however, I'll write to you
now because they might be a key for you. I wanted to write
that my work consists of two parts: of the one which is
here, and of everything which I have not written. And
precisely this second part is the important one.*

## I

The apophatic way, that's what you chose.
It's what you put in simpler words to Paul,
Your friend Paul Engelmann, so they'd disclose
The gist to one sufficiently in thrall
To your much-touted genius yet, as shows
In how you phrase it, one on whom they'd fall,
Your words, as enigmatically as those
Of Jesus. He must surely have brought small
Assurance to disciples in the throes
Of doubt or waning faith by his hardball
Return-shot parables that often pose
An obstacle to faith, or sheer brick wall.
The message says: your pleading merely goes
To show that faith's what's needed first of all,
Before the listener-out for it yet knows
How faithful ears can harken to its call.

## II

Your young disciple Engelmann's the one
Who took it on for you, that role assigned
To neophytes, word-spreaders, those who run

The 'life and legend' side of things, or find
Themselves a modest moment in the sun
By turning up some letter left behind
In desk or archive. There, the Master's spun
A tale that exegetes can bring to mind,
Like scriptural glossators, when they've done
With exegetic toils and feel inclined
To lend some credence to the myth begun
By his, the Master's, having once enshrined
It in a missive they'd most likely shun
As anecdotal stuff, though close-entwined,
Thereafter, in a narrative that none
Could junk once more judiciously streamlined.

### III

'Whereof we cannot speak, thereof should we
Keep silent' – wise advice, since any chat
On suchlike topics would turn out to be,
I fear, so like what those who chew the fat
On 'themes from Wittgenstein' regard as key
To figuring out just what he's getting at,
Or by what duly tacit process we
Loyal members of the commentariat
Can join that talkative conspiracy
Of hush. Then, as with Carroll's Cheshire Cat,
We're left with just the grin, the trace that he,
The Cat or Ludwig, take to signal that,
If we've received their joint epiphany,
We'd best believe the feline apophat:
'Here saying's out and showing's in to bat'.
Else what's unspoken proves a silent plea
That speech resume its living habitat,
Words cease to honour that perverse decree,

And commentators heed the caveat
That says (and shows) how sense and gravity
Alike keep that cat firmly on the mat.

# 8 Barren heights, green valleys

*Never stay up on the barren heights of cleverness, but*
*come down into the green valleys of silliness.*

Yes, there's some nonsense touted on the heights,
And wisdom to be had in valleys green,
Though sticking to the valleys may invite
A thought-conducive change of language-scene.

Else thinking may abstain from heady flights
But fall into the form-of-life routine
Confirmed each time your valley-dweller cites
Some language-game as 'how it's always been'.

Tough luck that Ludwig, he who should by rights
Have had his way and shucked them off, those keen
Epigones, should now have acolytes
As many as some star of stage and screen.

One thing they do provide, those 'barren heights
Of cleverness', is thoughts that intervene
And give all his like-minded neophytes
Or valley-folk some new ideas to glean.

For once a set of language-games unites
Those folk in forms of life long shared between
All parties, whence the new thought that excites
Resistance, theory-change, the slate wiped clean?

# 9 On linguistic bewitchment

*Philosophy is a battle against the bewitchment of our intelligence by means of language.*

No battles fierce as battles waged within,
Those psychomachias of the tortured soul,
As you, St. Ludwig, strove to salve the sin
Of language wrenched from communal control.

Your torment: the accord-disruptive spin
Of language-games that shunned their proper role
As bond-sustainers and their origin
In our (read: your) shared usage-protocol.

Else what could your words do but so bewitch
Your own and other folks' intelligence
That wayward utterances might soon unhitch
Their high gyrations from all ties of sense?

For it's that same intolerable itch
For verbal play that has you thus condense
Your gist in metaphors you'd have us ditch
Lest language-holidays should re-commence.

Yet shed the motley, go without a stitch
Of figural display, and you'll dispense
With all that tuned your readers to that pitch
Of Mardi Gris and Lenten penitence.

# 10 Human Body and Human Soul

*The human body is the best picture of the human soul.*

And so with you, St. Ludwig, so with you,
Whose soul – austere, ascetic – stands revealed
In snaps hand-picked by pupils, fit though few,
To show what vulgar reportage concealed.

A 'picture', maybe icon, maybe cue
For them, those first memorialists, to wield
Their own ascetic priesthood and accrue
Soul's lineaments as metempsychic shield.

That college room befits the picture too:
Sparse furnishings, the decor patched and peeled,
The image of a soul exposed to view
By souls responsive to its hermit yield.

What else was the compulsion that so drew
Those deck-chaired souls to him but what appealed
So strongly to apostles who well knew
Their vow to inner martyrdom thus sealed?

# 11 Pain and Language

*You learned the concept 'pain' when you learned language.*

The sufferer says: 'ah, there you go again,
Still on about those language-games you seem
To think are all we've need of to explain
Some cry of agony or sudden scream.

Your followers say you had your share of pain,
The psychic sort, but how should that redeem
What sounds to us like *d'haut en bas* disdain
For what disrupts your placid concept-scheme?

Small wonder if that regular refrain
Of yours, that anti-'private language' theme,
Should have us silent sufferers complain
And you sink bottom-ward in our esteem.

It's those that opt for doctrines so arcane
And shelter in austerity's regime
Who can, like you, quite placidly maintain
That thesis to absurdity's extreme.

Know, then, that nothing cuts against the grain
Of ordinary speech, that soothing dream,
Like one sharp spasm that derails the train
Of thought or halts the flow of words mid-stream.

So should some 'form of life' at length ordain
You its St. Ludwig, take one for the team
But think, as flames grow high or arrows rain:
'No word or concept fits that "pain"-lexeme'.

# 12 I don't know my way about . . . .

*A philosophical problem has the form: I don't know my way about.*

'The world is everything that is the case',
You said, but what's 'the case' for you turns out
To be some language-game that maps the space
Where you, perplexed, don't know your way about.

The language-problem, one you'll have to face
In its most taxing form since what you tout
As 'language' threatens to erase all trace
Of town, street, church, or landmark which your route

(US pronunciation) takes to base
Its travels on and risk no further bout
Of word-bewildered wandering where each pace
Meets *faux amis* you could have done without.

OK, dear Ludwig: not some kind of race
For quickest journey-time, yet why pile doubt
On doubt by having language thus embrace
A creed where word-to-world's such a far shout?

# 13 Giving philosophy peace

*The real discovery is one that enables me to stop doing*
*philosophy when I want to. The one that gives philosophy*
*peace, so that it is no longer tormented by questions which*
*bring itself into question.*

Well yes, we take your point: there's some who ought
To take it more to heart, make it their creed
And self-disintricate from webs of thought
Where flies may buzz once from their bottle freed.

Still there's the brusque but bracing quick retort:
What if your language-therapy should need,
To back it up, whole libraries left short
Of shelf-space, whole great forests left de-treed?

Truth is, dear Ludwig, those wise things you taught
Had all the commentariat agreed
That, lest untutored readers should distort
Your message, they be shown how best to read

Such gnomic dicta with the full support
Of specialists whose works are guaranteed
To throw up further issues of the sort
Beloved of those with families to feed.

And so the exegetes contrive to thwart,
By their excess, the very purpose he'd
Announced, although in words that seem to court
Such services despite the case they'd plead.

# 14 Knowledge and Acknowledgment

*Knowledge is in the end based on acknowledgment.*

And yet, and yet . . . so many sources call
Attention, if reluctantly, to your
Not having lived by that advice at all,
Or guessed what sad conclusions they might draw.

Self-unacknowledged, constantly they fall
From your censorious lips, the words that score
A knock-out, putdown, insult, chance to maul
Some shamefaced victim, or just wipe the floor

With those who'd opt to funk a verbal brawl
And so stay silent rather than ignore,
Like you at times, the writing on the wall
That spells: no holds barred in this time of war!

No question, your mere presence cast a pall
On social gatherings where you might deplore,
As once you had, a budding pianist's gall
In playing for your tortured ears once more

A piece you'd heard in some great concert-hall
Performed by some great player, but now bore
With mounting wrath until the long-feared squall
Broke on her like a Titan's *pas encore*.

Acknowledgment? What of the friends you'd bawl
Out, mock, or punish mercilessly for
Each failure – or refusal – to play ball
In language-games with you as comprador.

Too bad you held them totally in thrall,
And still do, those who'd yet stand guarantor
Of your acknowledging the simple call
That common creaturehood requires we shore

Against the loss of human wherewithal
That comes of thinking's failure to restore
The speaking body, poker-threats and all,
To its chief role at social being's core.

# 15 'I' and Language

*One of the most misleading representational techniques in our language is the use of the word 'I.'*
*Freud's fanciful pseudo-explanations (precisely because they are brilliant) perform a disservice. (Now any ass has these pictures available to use in 'explaining' symptoms of an illness.)*

'*Le moi est haïssable*': so it appears
You, Ludwig, share the sentiment expressed
So succinctly by Blaise Pascal, whose fears
Of ego's terrors you thus manifest.

It's as if ego haunts its own frontiers,
Patrols itself like border-guards obsessed
With tracking down the sound that strikes their ears
Like 'I' lamenting under house-arrest.

Your 'I's a world-horizon that enspheres
Not only ego's realm but – way out West –
The coastline glimpsed when ego's mist-bank clears
And language brings to view things long repressed.

You don't think much of Freud, but testy jeers
Betray misgivings: why not let the test
Be Id's odd way of paying its arrears
To Schopenhauer – so grudgingly redressed!

Think how your own first-person pronoun veers
From topping self's account to reinvest
Its balance in the slippage that careers
Along the meaning-chain, and then – no rest

For hapless ego! – lets them in, your fears
That maybe Freud's dark insights serve us best
If we're to grasp what he, St. Ludwig, hears
In those *unheimlich* gaps as host turns guest.

We hear them too who come to you with ears
Now finely tuned to catch them, whether blessed
Or cursed by tidings from our earliest years
To which, like you, we've suddenly regressed.

Who else, the rogue collocutor who steers
Your wiser self off-track so you're possessed
By demon doubts until a shift of gears
Or language-games requires they stay abreast

Of rules drawn up to see that thought adheres
To common usage lest infractions messed
With your assurance that those mutineers
Need pose no threat to our, or your, night's rest.

# 16 Doors: pushing and pulling

*A man will be imprisoned in a room with a door that's*
*unlocked and opens inwards; as long as it does not occur*
*to him to pull rather than push.*

Keep pushing, Ludwig, and you'll bust a gut.
Try pulling, and you'll soon be out of there.
The answer's plain enough, open-and-shut,
With doors and latches kept in good repair.

You thought 'hinge propositions' made the cut,
Brought certainty enough, and served to bear
Whatever weight was placed upon them, but
Left thoughts, like doors, some elbow room to spare.

Not, maybe, such a philosophic nut
For you to crack, the door thing, yet have care:
Those hinges are just waiting for some mutt
To barge through, scattering hinge-bits everywhere.

# 17 Spade and Bedrock

*If I have exhausted the justifications, I have reached*
*bedrock and my spade is turned. Then I am inclined to*
*say: 'This is simply what I do'.*

Yes, Ludwig, fair enough if that's your trade;
Keep digging, tell the world 'it's what I do',
And only when that bedrock meets your spade
Move on to try another dig or two.

Still there's the question whether you've not made,
As happens rather frequently with you,
A choice of metaphor that's not quite played
The plain sense-making role you meant it to

Since that's the 'bedrock' that you call in aid
As graphic instance of the credit due
To 'forms of life' or 'language-games' assayed
And found to fit our uses like a shoe.

Yet think: how should the custom-woven braid
Of human need and meaning drive askew
The downward thrust of that earth-cleaving blade
As if the mesh could block its passage through?

If 'call a spade a spade' has scarce been paid
The care it takes to have your thoughts run true
And not show your choice metaphors now frayed
Around the edges, then why still pursue

The notion that has language-games arrayed,
If only metaphorically, to strew
Across the path of any thought-parade
So spade-like that it longs to hack and hew?

No metaphor but has to make the grade
Conceptually if it's not to eschew
Philosophy's prime task, and so evade
The thought: so, Gorgias, what else is new?

# 18 Crazier than the philosophers

*It's only by thinking even more crazily than philosophers
do that you can solve their problems.*

A proper caucus race, this going crazy!
No rules, or make them up – the Dodo's game.
The nonsense/sense distinction soon gets hazy
But, hell, they all win prizes just the same!

No chance the gamy chancers might get lazier,
Not with such punter-boggling odds to tame.
The pile-ups are enough to give Scorsese a
Head-ache just to get them in the frame.

Puts you in mind of Wittgenstein: the mazier
His language-games, or more oblique his aim,
The fewer your exit-points from that fantasia
Of language-therapy that bears his name.

And once she's through the looking-glass, no glazier
To re-invert the way her world became
When Alice, Dodo-hooked, herself grew crazier
Than Ludwig with his up-the-ante claim.

# 19 Socrates and time-wasting

*Reading the Socratic dialogues one has the feeling: what a frightful waste of time!*

*What's the point of these arguments that prove nothing and clarify nothing?*

I

Well Ludwig, there's this thing called dialogue
Where different speakers put forward different views,
Mostly conflicting ones, and none can hog
The chat-time or in suchlike ways abuse

The rules to keep the others all agog
For their next speech, or lob some false *j'accuse*
In craftily so its effects will dog
The stricken party and ensure they lose

The slanging-match, or cunningly leapfrog
Some valid counter-argument and choose
Rhetorical low blows that let them slog
It out with not a care for what ensues.

II

But then, you've your . . . let's not say handy fools
Or useful idiots, but those who serve
As inner students whom the master schools
To show a slow but steady learning-curve

While you, that master, inculcate the rules
And – one chief topic – teach them to observe
What following them means, and suchlike jewels
Best gained through slant instruction, swerve by swerve.

## III

Yet, Ludwig, it's not hard to see why you'd
Find nothing useful, 'proved', or 'clarified'
By those Socratic disputants who hewed
To stricter rules, consented to abide

By dialectic's protocol, and viewed
With clearly marked disfavour any slide
Toward the Thrasymachian attitude
That has brute force, not reason, on its side.

Think, too, how little truth-sustaining food
For thought he, Socrates, would find supplied
By those mock-dialogues in which you brood
On your concerns and either praise or chide

The nameless sub-personae who include
A speaker for each soon-to-be-belied
Since dead-end line of argument pursued
By those whose views your own must override.

## IV

So: really not a dialogue in that
Socratic sense where parties all contend
On equal terms and each comes in to bat
With every hope of having, by the end,

At least conveyed what they were aiming at,
Made points the listeners-in could comprehend,
And, Socrates-like, raised the tone from chat,
Through conversation, to what might transcend

Their day-to-day affairs. So they'd be sat,
Indoors or out, engaging friend-to-friend
In talk that then required no change of hat
For 'high' philosophy because they'd lend

The same attentive ear in chew-the-fat
Exchanges. Thus no party would suspend
The civic-citizenly concordat
That urged dissenters to speak up, not blend

Then have one voice exert a caveat,
Like yours, that begs the errant pupil mend
His thinking, get the master's views off-pat,
Yet save appearances: no knee to bend!

# 20 How Frazer got it wrong?

*Burning in effigy. Kissing the picture of one's beloved...*
*it aims at nothing at all; we just behave this way and then*
*we feel satisfied.*
*Frazer's account of the magical and religious views of*
*mankind is unsatisfactory; it makes these views look*
*like errors.*

Odd how extremely keen you are to spurn
All those purported gifts we moderns preen
Our goodselves on while touting a return
To customs only fit for Hallowe'en.

If having our foes' effigies to burn
Is good as killing them, then they'll be keen
We keep the practice up, not get to learn
How primitive our folk-beliefs have been.

By all means kiss her picture when you yearn
For your beloved's presence, but come clean:
No man so primitive he won't discern
The difference when there's no such gap between.

You've got it in for Frazer, and your spleen,
St. Ludwig, has about it all the stern
Demeanour of the witch-pricker who'd lean
To fire as what those Devil's spawn should earn.

It's there in all the photographs, your mien
Of Chief Inquisitor who'll now adjourn
To see what further details he can glean
Of stuff the midnight witches used to churn.

Just give me Frazer, spare me those obscene
Barbarities, let no more victims burn,
And seek no latest pretext to convene
The holy ghouls with yet more bones to quern.

# 21 Kicking the ladder away

*My propositions are elucidatory in this way: he who*
*understands me finally recognizes them as senseless, when*
*he has climbed out through them, on them, over them. (He*
*must so to speak throw away the ladder, after he has*
*climbed up on it.)*

The ladder-kicking thing's all very well
For builders late turned stunt-men but sits ill
With thinkers itching to play merry hell
When others' claims have missing rungs to fill.

Good rule for novelists, that 'show, not tell'
Injunction Henry James made standard drill,
But not so good when arguments don't gel
And propositions fall out as they will.

Your novelist has ample leave to dwell
On details, scenes or characters as skill
Or plot demand, but thinkers need to spell
Their case out step-wise, like an invoice-bill,

If they're to make it good and so compel
Our rational assent, not merely spill
A heap of striking images pell-mell.
For them, the logophobic types to swill.

That's just where your *Tractatus* must excel,
That book of incantations, each a thrill
For koan-hungry readers who'd rebel
At being fed them through the logic-mill.

Yet, Ludwig, a philosopher should quell
Such feelings in himself lest they instil
The mystic's yen to chasten or expel
Whatever thoughtful check produced that chill.

For how should you, from the scholastic cell
Of what they call your life, think to fulfil
Those errant impulses that once befell
You like a devil snatching at your quill?

# 22 Meaning and use

*The meaning of a word is its use in the language.*
*Don't ask for the meaning; ask for the use.*

I

Look not for meanings, just look for the use.
There's risks involved in asking what things mean.
Don't set them thinking you've a thought-screw loose.

Else they'd say 'Come on, getting too abstruse –
There's lines to just read out, not read between.
Look not for meanings, just look for the use'.

Best not show too much hermeneutic *nous*
Lest sense-custodians should intervene.
Don't set them thinking you've a thought-screw loose.

It's *verbum sat sapienti*: plain obtuse
If thoughts acute bring outcomes unforeseen.
Look not for meanings, just look for the use.

Too bad if what you chase is some wild goose
That honks 'dive deeper, break the sense-routine!'.
Don't set them thinking you've a thought-screw loose.

Above all, don't provoke the wrath of Zeus
With auguries beyond man's wit to glean.
Look not for meanings, just look for the use;
Don't set them thinking you've a thought-screw loose.

## II

Best not enquire too deeply, hermeneut!
They'll blight your life whose interdict you break.
Going sub-surface? Check your diving-suit.

The child knows what they're at: 'Stay sweet, stay cute,
Just cut the whys and wherefores, for God's sake!'.
Best not enquire too deeply, hermeneut.

The adult too: 'you think you're so astute?
Tread water or you'll feel the seabed shake.
Going sub-surface? Check your diving-suit.

Just think what disincentives go to mute
The verdict: 'these appearances are fake'.
Best not enquire too deeply, hermeneut.

By censor's velvet glove or iron boot
They've ways to warn 'state interests at stake'.
Going sub-surface? Check your diving-suit.

Else dig down to the nethermost tap-root
Where your spade turns and leaves one choice to make:
Best not enquire too deeply, hermeneut;
Going sub-surface? Check your diving-suit.


## III

Dark secrets spring to view, turn but a stone.
Close-guarded for our common good they lie.
Trust teacher, leave those meanings well alone.

Please note this teacher's take-your-medicine tone:
Iron fist in velvet glove, no asking why.
Dark secrets spring to view, turn but a stone.

Keep asking and it's yours, the cover blown,
Not theirs – or its – the needful alibi.
Trust teacher, leave those meanings well alone.

He'll lay them down, the limits of the known,
Just tip the wink discreetly: 'best not pry'.
Dark secrets spring to view, turn but a stone.

For – trust St. Ludwig – faith's most truly shown
By prayerful speech that asks for no reply.
Trust teacher, leave those meanings well alone,

Or mark it 'Fear to Tread', that danger-zone
Where meaning-ransackers with plain sense vie.
Dark secrets spring to view, turn but a stone.

Then let him see how used to it you've grown
Who cringe beneath the sense-enforcer's eye.
Trust teacher, leave those meanings well alone;
Dark secrets spring to view, turn but a stone.


IV

Look to the use, you say; let meanings be!
Ah, but the use most often *is* what's meant.
No use but meaning must provide a key.

Just turn that stone, then tell us: what's to see
But meanings, senses, tokens of intent?
Look to the use, you say; let meanings be.

You'd have the meanings pass inspection-free,
Their use recruit us to its suasive bent.
No use but meaning must provide a key.

'Dad, what's this word mean, "ideology"?'
'No matter, son – your wondering's time ill-spent:
Look to the use, I say; let meanings be.'

'It must mean something, Dad, if not to me!'
'Look son, that word's plain useless – no dissent!'.
'Won't do, Dad – meaning must provide a key,

And Ludwig's bought right into it if he
Thinks the 'I'-word lacks sense or referent.
"Look to the use", he says; "let meanings be".
No use but meaning must provide a key.'

# 23 Subject, world, and what is the case

*The subject does not belong to the world, but it is a limit of the world.*

*The world is all that is the case.*

*Philosophy ought really to be written only as a form of poetry.*

### I

Ah yes, the world, 'all that's the case': let's junk
All that old stuff the thinkers used to fuss
So endlessly about – medieval bunk
Like metaphysics, things they'd once discuss

In deadly earnest, like some hefty chunk
Of Kantian critique that might nonpluss
The expert Kantians, or some book-length hunk
Of philosophic twaddle aimed to truss

Those thinkers up in knots until they've thunk
The better of it, read you, come to sus
The whole thing out, and seen its remnants shrunk
To ruins best viewed from a tourist bus.

### II

Well, that's your angle on it, Ludwig, yet
That angle's maybe premised on what are,
To say the least, assumptions still beset
By doubts you – doubtless truly – find bizarre,

Though Kant & Co. would surely not have let
Your case go through with the admission-bar
Fixed so far down that the base standard met
By yours would come up short of theirs by far.

Just ask what deeper insight we might get
From 'world is what's the case', and feel it jar,
That truism, with how we own a debt
Of thanks to those, like Kant, who rightly star

Not so much for the honours they might net
As plain truth-tellers but as on a par
With thinkers-through resolved not to abet
Such proppers-up of error's repertoire.


### III


But ask 'what is the case' *sub specie*
*Aeternitatis*, or in that remote
Since abstract 'world' invoked by your array
Of numbered propositions, and we'll float,

Like Swift's Laputan sages, clean away
From Wittgenstein's Vienna where he wrote
Some parts of the *Tractatus*, tried to say
What must be shown, not said, and struck that note

Of sibylline detachment that would play
Its role in having exegetes devote
Such endless labours to the task that they
Pursued through essay, tome, and anecdote.

# IV

And then, what of that same Vienna where
(Think 1930s, gathering storm, the rise
Of Fascism, a world *entre deux guerres*)
He, Ludwig, wrote the text that would comprise,

For him and others, thoughts that did their share
To conjure up, beyond those sullen skies,
A world austere as his, a room as bare
As his in Cambridge, and – to the surprise

Of Russell, Moore, and Co. – a certain flair
For gnomic utterances whose thin disguise
As *more geometrico* gives their
Interpreters a chance to exercise

Their hermeneutic talents with an air
Of privileged intuitive surmise
Or direct revelation vouched to spare
Them any sticking-points to analyse.

# V

You said it once, let drop a thought since then
Much dwelt upon by commentators whose
Chief aim is to display their acumen
As true close-readers anxious not to lose

This opportunity to turn their pen
To matters philosophical, peruse
That text so cherished by the frontiersmen
Of analytic rectitude, and cruise

The tractable *Tractatus*. It's their yen
For any hitherto unnoticed cues
Beyond the abstract concept-dealers' ken
But theirs to tap for ample revenues

Of all that's subtly conjured from it when
Close-read by critics keen to pay their dues
And really twist the exegetic screws –
Like Empson on George Herbert once again!


## VI

But then the thought occurs: if your idea –
One shared by many in that German line
Of cultural descent – requires we hear
In poetry what prose must needs consign

Beyond its bounded, vision-blocking sphere
Of reason, truth and logic, then that's fine
For literary folk who tend to veer
From such unhomely zones. Yet, Wittgenstein,

It's not what one expects or wants to hear
From those whose avocation's more to shine
Some light in places where there might appear
Thoughts that transcend the limits they assign

As reason's avatars, yet conjure fear
Lest kindred thoughts should once more cross the Rhine.
That's what requires they draw the boundary clear
Against all vain endeavours to divine,

By supra-rational means, a truth the seer,
Or mystagogue, or demagogue of *Sein*
*Und Zeit* proclivities, could seize and steer
To ends more mischievously serpentine.

A prosaist's dictum, that one must adhere
To principles no reasoner should resign
When 'doing philosophy' – yet hold them dear
Just when 'poetic licence' may combine

With aphoristic flair to tell us we're
Like Kafka's leopards who'd invade the shrine
Once, twice, then at set intervals each year
Till the accustomed supplicants would pine

At any non-appearance and revere
Those rogue intruders as the sacred wine
Of revelation, spurning truth's small beer
As unpoetic, earthbound, anodyne.

# 24 Language and the limits of thought

*In order to be able to set a limit to thought, we should
have to find both sides of the limit thinkable (i.e. we should
have to be able to think what cannot be thought). It will
therefore only be in language that the limit can be set, and
what lies on the other side of the limit will simply be
nonsense.*

Rather than look at clouds from both sides now,
Why not try some such thought-experiment
With thought itself, I ask, and wonder how,

If not in language, one might orient
Oneself to best advantage and allow
The nonsense that resulted when one went

Beyond that language-limit to endow
Itself with all the force of an event,
Albeit one that, like a Trappist vow,

Acknowledged what no words could represent
Unless their falling silent was the tao
And nonsense thought's own limit-crossing bent?

# 25 Language on holiday

*Philosophical problems arise when language goes on holiday.*

Yes, Ludwig, but, you know, it's quite OK
To take some time off, head for some resort
Or just some mental space where 'holiday'
Is not the language-guardian's retort

To any language-user whose display
Of verbal creativity is thought
By them, the guardians, to show that they,
The gifted verbalists, are just the sort

To tempt poor *homo loquens* from the way
Of language-rectitude. They'll idly sport
With speech-act solecisms that make hay,
In turn, with all the customs that support

Our own capacity to think and say
What needed saying. Fine, but don't distort
The issue here: there's heavy costs to pay
If you neglect to state it as you ought,

The inventive language-user's right to stray
From rules adopted principally to thwart
Whatever s/he might venture to convey
Of precious freedoms that the Voldemort

In you would conjure us to keep at bay
Despite your gift for metaphors that court
Your own reproof yet break the grey-on-grey
Like dolphins glimpsed astern as they cavort.

# 26 The tool-box of language

*Think of the tools in a tool-box: there is a hammer, pliers,*
*a saw, a screwdriver, a rule, a glue-pot, nails and screws.*

*. . . The functions of words are as diverse as the functions*
*of these objects.*

I

Think, too, the box may have some secret drawer,
Compartment or false bottom where you'll find
More tools but of a less familiar kind,
Like certain words and phrases from that store

Of language-games you fettled fit for your
Specific purposes and left behind
For word-hooked gamesters of a kindred mind
To ring their changes on each metaphor.

Those special tools are what they're looking for,
The ephebes, when they find themselves inclined
To venture out beyond the bounds assigned
By common usage or the language-lore

That you, their chief exemplar, always swore
Expressly by since they'd be flying blind
(You cautioned) or just idling offshore
If word and use were too far misaligned.

## II

Still you found ways to sneak a look inside
That secret drawer, the tool-kit that could do
Such strictly off-the-cuff jobs as provide
The metaphors and parables that you,

In 'literary' mode, permit to guide
Your thought, and ours, in ways slightly askew
To customary usage. Here reside,
As in the secret box: a cross-thread screw

That oddly fits a cross-thread nut; a dried-
Up glue-pot with a special sort of glue
That, softened, might take tricky jobs in stride;
A pair of pliers, slightly out-of-true

Yet sure of grip when dextrously applied;
A screwdriver with blade that's apt to chew
Most screw-heads yet's the only one to slide
In tight with some. Then: those bent nails in lieu

Of picture-hooks plus hammer-heads cockeyed
Enough to drive them in, not have them slew
Or buckle; gap-toothed saws you set aside
Till friction craves some missing tooth or two;

And – home terrain! – those rules we should abide
As strictly by as fits the job in view,
From straight-edged rules to ones still bona fide
Where deviations may give skill its cue

For craftsmanship, or speakers cause for pride
In innovative uses that accrue
More vivid powers of utterance than those tried-
And-tested rules whose sticklers come to rue

Their having checked the tool-box yet not spied
The secret drawer and, sadly, joined the queue
Of strict rule-followers keen to override
Your every trip to language-pastures new.

### III

For, *Lieber* Ludwig, other tools may lie
Perhaps not quite so readily to hand
In any standard tool-box yet still vie
For users' choice when any high-street brand

Screwdriver, screw or hammer won't get by
For want of just those properties that stand
Just so far off beneath the common sky
Of tool-use or the language-socius spanned

By rules so commonplace that they'd deny,
If stuck to, all but the commonest, most bland
Of speech-acts, or all brave attempts to try
The limits of invention. These expand

The secret drawer till spin-offs multiply,
Become what makes a 'standard' tool-box, and,
In time, what most would come to classify
As progress, whether hit upon or planned.

## IV

With your texts, too, the passages that tend
To get most quoted, be most widely shared,
Stick deepest in most minds, are those that bend
The rules a bit, show us you're quite prepared

To lift them for a moment and suspend
Our need to check that every utterance squared
With one or other language-game whose blend
Of custom and plain-speaking kindly spared

Linguistic reprobates from the false friend
Of games gone extra-communal that snared
Them in such high gyrations as must end,
Like Icarus, regretting all they'd dared.

## V

My point, again: they get it wrong who lend
Excessive credence to your self-declared
Reliance on the handsome dividend
Enjoyed by language-users who've not cared

To risk the mental costs they apprehend
As consequent on ideas gamely aired
By over-reachers itching to transcend
Mere communal accord. What brightly flared

When Icarus so briefly bucked the trend
And worsted gravity was how they've erred,
The exegetes, in having you commend
Plain speech as recourse from the perils bared

In your foredoomed attempt to somehow fend
It off, the poet's gift that had you scared
To acknowledge in yourself the overspend
Of verbal creativity impaired

At times but never quelled as they'd pretend,
The Wittgensteinians unsure just where'd
It break through next, your proneness to up-end
A tool-box shut on language-games unshared.

# 27 . . . a picture held us captive . . .

*A picture held us captive. And we could not get outside it, for it lay in our language and language seemed to repeat it to us inexorably.*

*One of the most misleading representational techniques in our language is the use of the word 'I'.*

I

No more than that, a conjurer's technique.
'First person singular' – my alibi!
Ask who's at home, and you'll have far to seek.

Mauthner was right in this – it's *Sprachkritik*
We need if we're to exorcise the 'I'.
No more than that, a conjurer's technique.

'Shifter', 'deictic', 'token-reflexive' – peek
At those linguistic workings on the sly,
Ask who's at home, and you'll have far to seek.

High time the soul cast off that old mystique,
Along with this hard truth it would deny:
No more than that, a conjurer's technique.

I feel it happening each time I speak,
That 'I' whose words re-echo, multiply . . . .
Ask who's at home, and you'll have far to seek.

Too deep the language-picture goes, too weak
The ego-solvents language has me try.
No more than that, a conjurer's technique.
Ask who's at home, and you'll have far to seek.


II


Not merely mine, that picture, mine alone.
What chance salvation were it merely mine,
Joint prisoner and gaoler, each his own?

It's by shared language-games we self-atone.
See Crusoe teach Man Friday, sign-by-sign!
Not merely mine, that picture, mine alone.

*Le penseur* gnaws upon no toothsome bone
But chews and broods as tail/tongue-waggers dine.
Joint prisoner and gaoler, each his own.

Yet where if not in language is it shown
How deep the picture lies, how bottom-line?
Not merely mine, that picture, mine alone.

Those fellows, Moore and Russell, say I've grown
Too introvert – 'do cheer up, Wittgenstein'.
Joint prisoner and gaoler, each his own,

I tell them, 'self-imprisoned, picture-prone,
Crusoe un-Fridayed – otherwise I'm fine!'.
Not merely mine, that picture, mine alone;
Joint prisoner and gaoler, each his own.

## III

All have their pictures; mine spells 'solipsist'.
I spurn it, plead 'it's language-games we share'.
Each time the picture answers: 'plea dismissed!'.

One aim in all I write: to turn its gist
Back smartly, intercept it in mid-air!
All have their pictures; mine spells 'solipsist'.

'A saintly type', they'll say, 'no egoist',
Then add: 'though often lost in private prayer'.
Each time the picture answers: 'plea dismissed'.

How should I ever make a decent fist
Of it, this language-game played solitaire?
All have their pictures; mine spells 'solipsist'.

How should a private language-game not twist
What social sense my utterance might bear?
Each time the picture answers: 'plea dismissed'.

Games should commune, not merely coexist,
Else who'll relieve the castaway's despair?
All have their pictures; mine spells 'solipsist'.
Each time the picture answers: 'plea dismissed'.


## IV

Sometimes I think 'I' holds you captive too.
A savage irony might let you see
We're desert-islanded, the me and you.

An archipelago, each shipwrecked crew
Of loners joined in Hobbesian comity.
Sometimes I think 'I' holds you captive too.

You watch me closely, hoping for some clue
To 'what goes on inside', some psychic key.
We're desert-islanded, the me and you.

Inside my picture I've this 'I'-framed view
Of you Leibnizian monads watching me.
Sometimes I think 'I' holds you captive too.

See how the exegetes observe me through
The 'I'-frame matched to my observatory.
We're desert-islanded, the me and you.

My texts have brought it off, that master-coup
Of transference that grips each inductee.
Sometimes I think 'I' holds you captive too;
We're desert-islanded, the me and you.

### V

They'll say 'he loved the movies, cheapest seats,
Frequented flea-pits, gorged on silver screen'.
The image moves; the 'I'-frame just repeats.

'Love slumming it, those high-brow male elites;
Low dive, high table – splendid change of scene!'.
They'll say 'he loved the movies, cheapest seats'.

Truth is, the moving picture clearly beats
That static, thought-arresting word-machine.
The image moves; the 'I'-frame just repeats.

Sometimes, perplexed, I'll walk the Cambridge streets
Till Chaplin's gestures show me what I mean.
They'll say 'he loved the movies, cheapest seats'.

It's at such moments cinema defeats
Thought's stasis by a movement quick and clean.
His image moves; the 'I'-frame just repeats.

When Fairbanks pulls a stunt his act entreats
The Moores and Russells: jump your thought-routine!
They'll say 'he loved the movies, cheapest seats'.
The image moves; the 'I'-frame just repeats.


## VI


'Deep in our language that false picture lay.'
I said as much, knew where to place the blame.
What if some fault of mine led me astray?

I dismissed Freud in my accustomed way,
Declared his, too, a faulty language-game:
'Deep in our language that false picture lay'.

Yet 'Ludwig's in denial', so he'd say,
And back my old misgivings quickly came:
What if some fault of mine led me astray?

Too long, perhaps, I held such doubts at bay
And kept good friends' rebukes outside the frame.
'Deep in our language that false picture lay',

I told them still, but knew there'd come a day
When proofs piled up to falsify the claim.
What if some fault of mine led me astray?

That lady pianist whom I once heard play,
And badly! – still, to walk out – cause for shame.
'Deep in our language that false picture lay' –

The statement strikes me now as one that they,
Those friends, had better not cite in my name.
What if some fault of mine led me astray?
Perhaps deep in myself that picture lay.

# 28 Wittgenstein, Gödel, Turing

*There is no religious denomination in which the misuse of metaphysical expressions has been responsible for so much sin as it has in mathematics.*

*Even when all the possible scientific questions have been answered, the problems of life remain completely untouched.*

*Mathematical propositions express no thoughts. In life it is never a mathematical proposition which we need, but we use mathematical propositions only in order to infer from propositions which do not belong to mathematics to others which equally do not belong to mathematics.*

## I

They got me wrong, those Vienna Circle fools,
Made me the sage of their pathetic clique.
What do they know of logic and its rules?

They'd have me shuttlecock between two stools,
The logic-chopper and the saintly freak.
They got me wrong, those Vienna Circle fools.

Schlick, Carnap, Moritz and their propagouls –
For them I switched personae week-to-week.
What do they know of logic and its rules?

How subtly my *Tractatus* ridicules
The formal protocols they'd vainly seek!
They got me wrong, those Vienna Circle fools.

As logic falters my dark thread unspools
And leaves naught meaningful for them to speak.
What do they know of logic and its rules?

Soon I'd see concepts, thoughts and words as tools
To fix confusions as you'd fix a leak.
They got me wrong, those Vienna Circle fools;
What do they know of logic and its rules?

## II

I curse myself who played their logic-game,
Then left them like some Buddhist avatar.
Too devious, too Gödel-like my aim.

He turned up once, stayed quiet, and never came
Again since his two proofs would likely jar.
I curse myself who played their logic-game.

'No proving logic sound', so ran his claim;
'No self-consistent truths – just how things are!'
Too devious, too Gödel-like my aim.

Still he devised that number-scheme to frame
A proof that pressed all proofs a step too far.
I curse myself who played their logic-game.

His proof-disproof worked out, yet all the same
Unfixed the logic-fanciers' fixed star.
Too devious, too Gödel-like my aim.

Of course by then I'd found a means to tame
The formal drive his proof would soon debar.
I curse myself who played their logic-game

Because their logic's just another name
For talk those anal types deem up to par.
Too devious, too Gödel-like my aim;
I curse myself who played their logic-game.


## III

I say: make language-games your bottom line;
Concede that at this point your spade is turned.
Keep clear of Gödel's Platonist cloud nine.

He thought with Plato's aid we could divine
His theorem's truth though logically unearned.
I say: make language-games your bottom line.

He'd have us somehow grasp those truths that shine
In Plato's sphere, by occult means discerned.
Keep clear of Gödel's Platonist cloud nine.

Poor Kurt: no surer way to undermine
The fame his incompleteness-proof had earned.
I say: make language-games your bottom line,

Not access to a realm that would combine
A mystic's dream with lessons stepwise learned.
Keep clear of Gödel's Platonist cloud nine.

Else it's the 'genius' billing you'll resign
For 'loony tune', by friends and colleagues spurned.
I say: make language-games your bottom line;
Keep clear of Gödel's Platonist cloud nine.


## IV


They do me wrong, the *mathematikoi*,
Conceive no game but theirs correctly played!
Place logic centre-stage, their usual ploy.

Gödel and Turing – I'm their whipping-boy,
Set up for rough stuff by the math-brigade.
They do me wrong, the *mathematikoi*.

Across the shooting-range of math *topoi*
And logic-stalls they ply their stock-in-trade,
Place logic centre-stage, the usual ploy.

Turing's the worst – quite unconcealed, his joy
In calling my mathematics learner-grade.
They do me wrong, the *mathematikoi*.

'A third-hand prophet, clutching his Tolstoy
And holding forth on how he's been betrayed.'
Place logic centre stage, the usual ploy,

Treat language as no more than logic's toy,
And caution my best students: 'don't be swayed'.
They do me wrong, the *mathematikoi*.

Not me, but all I stand for they'd destroy,
Whatever small advance I might have made.
Place logic centre-stage, the usual ploy;
They do me wrong, the *mathematikoi*.


V


They think that rules extend like rails of steel,
Stretch out inexorably, straight ahead,
No grounds for doubt, no judgement to appeal.

I told a fictive story to reveal
How far strict rule-enforcers are misled
Who think that rules extend like rails of steel.

'Keep adding n + 1, go on, just reel
Those + 1's off', the baffled teacher said:
'No grounds for doubt, no judgement to appeal'.

But one kid spotted Sir's Achilles' heel,
Came up with some more complex rule instead:
'He thinks that rules extend like rails of steel'.

And so the pupil spun new ways to deal
With any rule the teacher took as read:
'No grounds for doubt, no judgement to appeal'.

They call me crackpot yet routinely kneel
At teacher's feet, mind-groomed and rulebook-fed.
They think that rules extend like rails of steel;
No grounds for doubt, no judgement to appeal.

# VI

Who's then to say the stubborn pupil erred?
No rule so hard it holds all followers fast.
What holds for teacher is a practice shared.

'For "plus" read "quus"', the dissident declared,
'Then make "quus" mean what gets my answer passed.'
Who's then to say the stubborn pupil erred?

It's communal assent decrees he fared
Less well than others, that iconoclast.
What holds for teacher is a practice shared.

Yet teacher should have seen his answer squared
With how the quus-rule brought it out at last.
Who's then to say the stubborn pupil erred?

Mere prejudice if teacher's not prepared
At least to have the pupil's work re-classed.
What holds for teacher is a practice shared.

Gödel and Turing are just running scared
If such conclusions leave them both aghast!
Who's then to say the stubborn pupil erred?

At any rate they might back then have spared
My findings their ironic icy blast.
What holds for teacher is a practice shared;
Who's then to say the stubborn pupil erred?

65

# VII

Their label for me should come straight to hand,
My moniker, my Theophrastian tag:
'The Sophist', that disreputable brand.

Still, it's with Gorgias I'll take my stand
Rather than Socrates, that ceaseless nag!
Their label for me should come straight to hand.

Those Sophists were an undeluded band
Of language-gamers, word-tools packed in bag!
'The Sophist', that disreputable brand.

The *mathematikoi* would have me banned,
An enemy of reason, one to gag!
Their label for me should come straight to hand.

Yet language-gamers have the skill to land
A verbal point that brings a logic-snag.
'The Sophist', that disreputable brand!

Your rules contract thought's ambit, mine expand
Its scope as far as fluent tongues can wag.
Your label for me should come straight to hand.

It's like bypassing Descartes' pineal gland,
The cogito's redoubt, and saying 'flag
The Sophist, that disreputable brand!'.
Your label for me should come straight to hand.

## VIII

That some reproofs strike home I'll not deny.
Russell's now turned against me, and I grieve.
What fixed points should I set my compass by?

I tell myself: enough to certify
You speak aright that it's what folk believe.
That some reproofs strike home I'll not deny.

Quite true, as Russell says: it's a far cry
To truth from things I'd readily conceive.
What fixed points should I set my compass by?

His gossip broke our friendship, and yet I
Still look to him for – what? – my late reprieve?
That some reproofs strike home I'll not deny.

Still, one I can't explain – the question why
I'd keep that language-game card up my sleeve.
What fixed points should I fix my compass by?

Perhaps – who knows? – the same odd rules apply
Now as years back, in ways we can't retrieve.
That some reproofs strike home I'll not deny;
What fixed points should I set my compass by?


## IX

Prove proofs unprovable: the thing's absurd!
Rules, proofs, truth-tables – handy tools, no more.
What's there that language-games can't undergird?

Of course it's down to 'rule', that weasel-word.
Pressed hard, it's bound to hit some logic-flaw.
Prove proofs unprovable: the thing's absurd!

It's just that words like 'rule' have senses blurred
When used in contexts they're not suited for.
What's there that language-games can't undergird?

It's sense goes begging where the project's spurred
By mad conclusions they've set out to draw.
Prove proofs unprovable: the thing's absurd.

Poor Gödel, like some lately flightless bird
Still pondering what first made its flight-path yaw.
What's there that language-games can't undergird?

He chewed the branch he sat on, undeterred
When logic turned on thought with tooth and claw.
Prove proof unprovable: the thing's absurd!

They think in numbers, even as numbers herd
All thought into their watchword-crunching maw.
What's there that language-games can't undergird?
Prove proof unprovable: the thing's absurd!

X

Turing's to blame, him and his thought-machine!
The halting-problem: does it run and run?
It might, it mightn't – what more could this mean?

If theorems won't stand up, if they first lean
This way, then that, you're sure to jump the gun.
Turing's to blame, him and his thought-machine!

As language weakens, as our mental scene
Grows computational, so thought's undone:
It might, it mightn't – what more could this mean?

A vital requisite of thought-hygiene:
To spell things out before the wheel is spun.
Turing's to blame, him and his thought-machine,

For all those goings-on behind a screen
Where thought takes forms unknown to anyone.
It might, it mightn't – what more could this mean?

Perplexed, I think again how Augustine
Found words for life renewed – I've scarce begun!
Turing's to blame, him and his thought-machine,

Though just conceivably a man might glean
Some impetus from thoughts he'd rather shun.
It might, it mightn't – what more could this mean?
Turing's to blame, him and his thought-machine.

# 29 Trying to say the whole thing

*Each sentence that I write is trying to say the whole thing,*
*that is, the same thing over and over again and it is as*
*though they were views of one object seen from different*
*angles.*

Bill Empson, whom you knew, said don't despair:
The problems pile up as conditions change,
So best change with them, track their scope and range.

Seen from all angles, still those things declare
It's craving all-round views makes them look strange.
'You don't want madhouse and the whole thing there'.

*(Last line quoted from William Empson's cryptic 6-line*
*poem 'Let It Go'.)*

# 30 Showings: a double sestina

*If a person tells me he has been to the worst places I have*
*no reason to judge him; but if he tells me it was his*
*superior wisdom that enabled him to go there, then I know*
*he is a fraud.*

*The real discovery is the one which enables me to stop*
*doing philosophy when I want to. The one that gives*
*philosophy peace, so that it is no longer tormented by*
*questions which bring itself into question.*

The world is everything that is the case.
All that's the case is all that we can say.
Some things cannot be said but may be shown.
These are the most important things in life.
A change in them will be a change of world.
Let silence show where saying leads astray.

So many ways we can be led astray!
Delinquent speech is not the only case,
Though certain evils may infect our world
Through word-abuse. Believing we can say
What matters most, in language or in life,
Is Russell's error. This much can be shown.

That's why my faithful few won't have it shown
How moral compass-points can swing astray
Even with such ascetic forms of life
Or utterance as mine. Count it a case
Of things-gone-wrong that nobody could say
Belonged exclusively to word or world.

Russell and Moore: they were my Cambridge world
Back then although, despite some kindness shown,
They failed to grasp how using words to say
Those things unsayable led sense astray.
Their verdict on me: genius, but a case
Of life screwed up by mind and mind by life.

'Just tell them that it's been a wonderful life.'
My dying words, and spoken from a world
So distant, now, from all that is the case
With their world that what's said by them, or shown,
Will likely lead my auditors astray
As much as anything I've had to say.

Yet there's some truth in what the others say,
My critics, who'd regard a tortured life
Like mine as leading and as led astray
Since formed within the solipsistic world
Of my obsessions. That's the sole thing shown,
They'd say, by such a cautionary case.

I keep my life a closed book just in case
Some rogue biographer should have his say
And seek, for no good cause, to have it shown
That there were certain chapters in that life
Kept secret from the academic world
Lest scandal lead my acolytes astray.

Yet could it be some young men went astray
Because I'd cruise the Prater and then case
The gay joints in my craving for a world
As far removed as possible from, say,
The wealth and privilege of my old life,
Or the mixed spite and condescension shown

By Moore and his Apostles? If I've shown
A seamy side, a will to go astray
In quest of what they'll call 'his other life',
It's not (the vulgar-Freudian view) a case
Of my abject desire that they should say
Harsh things that show me up before the world

For what I am. Rather, I deem that world
Of theirs a world in need of being shown
Such truths as neither they nor I can say
Since, in the saying, sense would go astray
And make me out a monster or a case
For some corrective treatment. It's my life,

Not anything I've written, but my life
As lived that bears sole witness to the world
Concerning just those matters in the case
Of Ludwig Wittgenstein that should be shown,
Not said, since uttering them sends words astray
And has them mimic what they fail to say.

And yet I ask: why think of 'show' and 'say'
In such bi-polar terms unless your life,
Like mine, has gone unspeakably astray
And left you stranded in an alien world
Where your 'condition' can at most be shown,
Not talked about or stated, just in case.

A modest claim: to say, not save, the world,
Yet still too statement-bound, as life has shown.
What was it went astray with what's the case?
No world exists that logothetes might say
'Here's all we've shown: that words bring worlds to life'.
What if 'the case' just is what goes astray?

73

# 31 Doors and Pictures

*A picture held us captive. And we could not get outside it,
for it lay in our language and language seemed to repeat it
to us inexorably.*

*A man will be imprisoned in a room with a door that's
unlocked and opens inwards; as long as it does not occur
to him to pull rather than push it.*

*I think I summed up my attitude to philosophy when I said:
philosophy ought really to be written only as a poetic
composition.*

He had this thing about what you could say
   And what you couldn't say but only show.
To make the point, he thought, his only way
   Was to push 'say' as far as it would go.
With that in mind he'd put up an array
   Of reasonings *more geometrico*,
Along with a meticulous display
   Of numbered parts that made it seem as though
The thing was too well-built to go astray.
   This would ensure that those chaps in the know,
Bertie and his lot, had their role to play
   As dupes in Ludwig's stratagem to blow
A T-shaped hole in everything that they,
   Like his Tractarian double, took as so
Self-evident as strictly to convey
   No more than syllogistic might bestow
By way of sense or content. Yet dismay
   Set in when those same chaps proved far too slow

To take his point, or eager to essay
   Some risk-containment exercise that no
Depth-rumblings might disturb. This helped allay
   Their nagging sense that he'd contrived to stow
Something in his oblique communiqué
   That threatened to upset the status quo
Of language, truth, and logic. Anyway
   They picked it up, the cryptic undertow
In this strange work of Russell's protégé,
   But made sure it was kept so far below
Deck in the first translation as to stay
   Disarmed of any spanners it might throw
Into the works. For there they'd ricochet
   And cause no end of philosophic woe
To Russell and those heralds of the day
   When mystics would repay the debt they owe
To logic. Then they'd see fit to obey
   Such rational demands as bid them toe
No line where superstition's apt to prey
   On trust or faith says reason should forego
Its privilege. Keep saintliness at bay,
   His colleagues thought, lest worldly wit lie low
In deference to it and extend the sway
   Over weak minds of any holy joe
With some new crack-brained gospel to purvey,
   Or any US-style politico
With God on board. That stuff was now *passé*,
   So Russell thought, that Sunday-School tableau
Got up with all the faux-naiveté
   By which the firm of Jesus Christ & Co
Had managed so adroitly to portray
   Their potentate as power's most powerful foe.
Yet this ignored Saint Ludwig's *dieu caché*,
   His hidden god (think Pascal, think Godot),

75

Whose failure to arrive as promised may,
  To souls elect, reveal the vapid flow
Of saying's intellectual cabaret
  Struck dumb. Thus having nothing *à propos*
To say – and falling silent – might defray
  The cost of all those endless to-and-fro
Discussions spawned, he thought, by the decay
  Of what once found expression (think Rousseau)
In sentiments that showing might relay
  Once all the saying's done. On this plateau
The tribe of *bons sauvages* join Mallarmé
  In savouring only fragrances that blow
From flowers that have their place in no bouquet,
  Or hues that vanish in the gaslight glow
Of rainbows shadowed by the grey-on-grey
  That passes muster in the Savile Row
Of logic-suited thought. The first rule: pay
  No heed to anything we cannot sew,
Us stitchers-up, to standards checked OK
  For sticking to the proper ratio
Of words to thoughts and things lest words outweigh
  Truth's currency and thinking undergo
Such figural bewitchments as betray
  Its old malaise. His message: we should grow
Alert when language 'went on holiday'
  Since here it often held in embryo
All the misshapen progeny that lay
  Athwart the path to thinking's *vrai niveau*
Of common speech. Such were those *recherché*
  Linguistic idioms that he thought *de trop*
Since parasitic on the DNA
  Of communal accord, or the escrow
That underwrote our forms of everyday
  Folk-usage. This he showed us, *modulo*

The need for umpteen exegetes to say
    Just what it was his words were meant to show,
As witness the shelf-bending dossier
    Of monographs and endless *de nouveau*
Renditions of old themes whose overstay
    He'd hoped his *Tractatus* would long ago
Have laid to rest. Last irony: that they,
    His acolytes, should be the ones whom no
Strict rule, like his, against such making hay
    With words and concepts could persuade to throw
The habit off despite its threat to fray
    The bonds of communal accord and so
Permit such verbal licence (aka
    Delinquency) to twist the quid pro quo
That constitutes a true *communauté*
    *De langue et vie*. His tragedy: to know,
If dimly, that he'd pointed them the way
    And sounded the linguistic tallyho
That led his followers to a disarray
    Of language-games as likely to kayo
That prospect as the mutants on display
    In some linguistic isle where Doc Moreau
Spliced metaphors like genes. And so, *malgré*
    His dearest wish, this anti-Prospero
Saw monstrous life-forms bred out of Roget
    By language-games from his own portmanteau.

# 32 I, world and visual field

*Nothing in the visual field allows you to infer that it is seen by an eye.*

*There are no subjects in the world. A subject is a limitation of the world.*

*Our life is endless in the way that our visual field is without limit.*

*The philosophical I is not the man, not the human body or the human soul of which psychology treats, but the metaphysical subject, the limit – not a part of the world.*

I

True, Ludwig, but there's more to 'I' than 'eye'.
Almost one thinks 'here lurks an English pun:
First-person singular – a shifty spy!'.

The infant, Lacan's *hommelette,* can't apply
'Me', 'you', or 'she' because the contents run
And lose all clear distinction as they fry.

But gradually things start to clarify,
Self, mother, father, then the 'everyone'
Of those third-persons as they multiply.

And once that happens, time to say goodbye
To all the polymorphous-perverse fun
Of infancy and stage the self's first try

To frame at any rate an alibi
For some self-image of the mother's son
Or father's daughter able to say 'I',

Impersonate the grown-up gal or guy,
And carry on the process, once begun,
Of entering the Symbolic yet, thereby,

Relinquishing what now they must deny
Of infant *jouissance* – breast to sticky bun –
While *petit objet a* feigns reasons why.


## II

Ludwig, that eye of yours looks one decreed
To gaze out on a visual field defined
By nothing more than its, the eye's, own need

For privacy, seclusion, and – just read
Those epigraphs above! – a state of mind,
An 'I', determined now no more to heed

Your previous mentors, even those agreed,
Like Moore and Russell, that your special kind
Of genius must, by sheer compulsion, lead

You far beyond whatever guaranteed,
By their own lights, the certitudes behind
Their thinking, logic-led and progress-keyed.

Your 'I's a world entire whose bounds recede
Beyond all limits hitherto assigned
By those who'd likewise sought a locus freed

From Pascal's pesky *moi haïssable*. We'd
Much better – you imply – go aspect-blind
To much that makes us human, and, as he'd

Advise, consider man the 'thinking reed'
(Pascal again) whose frailties may yet find
Due compensation if we take your lead,

Blest anchorite, and let those frailties plead
Our case, we bare forked creatures disinclined
To have them spoil thought's vigil or impede

The process whereby every title-deed
To shared humanity is realigned
With all that vitiates our mortal breed.

### III

How else interpret that self-emptying
Of selfhood, subject, ego, mind, or soul,
That pure *askesis* which alone can bring –

At least in worlds where one-eyed man is king –
An omnipresent 'I' that fills the whole
Of space, and whose perimeter must ring

Or 'limit' any little part we'd cling
To finally. Else it might play the role
Of lifeworld for the one intent to fling

The rest away or view it on the wing
To those far bounds and so regain control
Of what some distant glimpse could always spring

To discompose the visual field and swing
Your errant eye to where the vagrant mole
Throws up new hills for your delimiting.


IV


That eye must have transfixed your pupils, caught
(Like you, no doubt) in the fly-bottle where
They gloss each word and buzz about each thought

You once let fall, ignoring all you taught
Concerning philosophical hot air,
The need to just stay silent when we've naught

Of consequence to say, the mischief wrought
By seeing things asquint while trapped in there,
As through a bottle darkly, and what ought

To give those pupils pause. It's how you sought,
Sincerely it would seem, to have them spare
The world new beds of thinking reeds distraught

With pseudo-problems of the very sort
That you, their sole begetter, deemed a snare
For those epigoni but never brought

Yourself quite to relinquish. Their retort:
The ceaseless books and articles that bear
Depressing witness to how masters thwart

Their own best wisdom when they thus resort
To chiding others for the ways they err
Themselves, the Daedalean falling-short

81

Of insights gained yet all too dearly bought.
Frankly, it shows you keener to prepare
Your trainee acolytes than lend support

To those who'd much prefer that you'd escort
Them from that lidless visual field whose glare
Pursues them with its magistral *mainmorte*.

# 33 Thinking: pen, head, music

*I really do think with my pen, because my head often
knows nothing about what my hand is writing.
Sometimes, in doing philosophy, one just wants to utter an
inarticulate sound.
I think I summed up my attitude to philosophy when I said:
philosophy ought really to be written only as a poetic
composition.
Schiller writes . . . of a 'poetic mood'. I think I know what
he means, I think I am familiar with it myself. It is the
mood of receptivity to nature and one in which one's
thoughts seem as vivid as nature itself.*

I

A curious business, this – head, hand and pen.
So close the link of pen with hand
As thought takes written shape; of hand with head
As words prompt thought still further; and
Of pen with thought's new bearing as it then
Strikes out for some yet unknown land
As if magnetically and triply sped
By conjoint exercise of head, hand, pen.

It's in and through my writing that those 'themes
From Wittgenstein' they speak of cease
To occupy my mind and, once again,
My written words somehow release
A kind of thinking that, at moments, seems
To find its source in ancient Greece,
Almost like Hölderlin, and touch a strain
Of sense beyond all mere philosophemes.

'There's really no way to philosophise
Except in poetry', I wrote,
Unwisely you might think since nothing irks
The Moores and Russells like that note
Of rapture struck when thinkers rhapsodize
Or poets run some garbled quote
From a philosopher which (they think) works
To give their thinker-ratings a quick rise.

Still, 'poetry' I said, and meant, although
The kind of poetry that he,
The Empson man, was writing – not the kind
Most people might deem 'poetry'
At all, but verse so intricate and so
Rewarding to philosophers like me
That it was just the sort I had in mind
When I made that remark, decades ago.


## II


I met the critic Leavis once in town
And asked him kindly to go through
An Empson poem for my benefit,
Which he therewith agreed to do
Yet, I thought, rather let the poem down –
Got the verse-basics right, it's true,
But overlooked the subtleties, the wit,
And all that might befit the scholar's gown.

What his account conspicuously lacked
Was any sense of how, beyond
The sacrosanct 'words on the page' and their
First-order sense, one might respond
With greater (let's say) hermeneutic tact
To that which, maybe, stretched the bond
Of a shared language-game yet by whose rare
Poetic gift its zones could interact.

He, Leavis, told this tale and scorned to edit
The awkward bit where I express
My perturbation at his having not
Done justice to the liveliness,
The grace, and – what so struck me as I read it –
The strength of intellect no less
For managing, as poets do, to spot
A chance to play the sage and take the credit.

Not mine, that overly conceited style
Of Empson's, but he does combine
Two things that lift true poetry above
Philosophy: the singing line
Of passions that, in others, might beguile
The thinker yet here bring the spine
Of man's 'erected wit' to make of love
A theme fit for the shrewdest logophile.

# III

I say 'not mine, that style', but then reflect:
How else describe those scraps retailed
By quoters, 'fans', disciples, exegetes,
Or thesis-writers who've just nailed
My life's-work down by way of fragments checked
Word-perfect but whose users failed
To ask if, trotted out like lines of Keats,
They echo Forster's plea: only connect!?

Unstring those pearls and you'll have readers strung
Unthinkingly along, betrayed
By passages that have, let's say, the feel,
The almost lyric charge conveyed
Or sense of depths unplumbed that's somehow clung
To those choice jottings, yet reveal
Small grasp of any thought-transitions made
Along the florid branch from which they're hung.

I like him, Empson, from the bit I've seen
Of him about town, and his verse
Which has me thinking: when I first let drop
These thoughts I meant to reimburse
The poets, him among them, who'd long been
My rescuers from Plato's curse,
His envy-bred demand that poets stop
Distorting the plain sense of what words mean.

There's that bit, too, where I remark how good
It might feel, sometimes, just to make
A loud, a gross, a sub-articulate noise
And thereby flout all it might take
To regain entry to the neighbourhood
Of sense and reason where we wake
Up, even so, to all the fears and joys
Of what he, Hölderlin, once understood

As spirit's earthly dwelling. There alone,
As Empson's wire-drawn poem shows,
Can intellect accede to the demand
That it and love make common cause
And open heart and mind to all that's known
Through their potential to disclose,
When language takes a self-revealing hand,
How often those verse-accents haunt my prose.

# 34 Back to the Rough Ground!

*We have got onto slippery ice where there is no friction*
*and so in a certain sense the conditions are ideal, but also,*
*just because of that, we are unable to walk. We want to*
*walk so we need friction. Back to the rough ground!*

*It is difficult to describe paths of thought where there are*
*already many paths laid down, and not fall into one of the*
*grooves.*

I

'Get off the ice, get back to the rough ground!
So fine those high ideals, but lest you slip
And break a bone, or rule, just take this tip:
Don't walk where points of friction can't be found.'

A thing with you, an image-cluster sure
To have some 'real-life' bearing quite aside
From how the self-same metaphor applied
To issues with some anecdotal lure.

Inviscid, incompressible, and – just
As fictive – irrotational: that's what
You need to postulate of fluids, not
As if such ideal constructs could or must

Exist in nature but because, if you're
A cutting-edge researcher, then you need
To use them as and when since it's agreed
They'll be reset or normalised once more.

Somehow you didn't get it, thought the gap
Between ideal and physical a scandal,
And one the scientists could only handle
By having better judgment take a nap.

And so with logic: where its crystalline
Perfection proved a less than perfect means
Of doing other stuff – no hill of beans
To most logicians who got on just fine

With its intrinsic limits – you professed,
Again, that sense of finding this a case
Where such accommodations have no place:
Those false ideals mean logic's flunked the test!


## II

Call me reductionist, but I detect,
In all those images and metaphors,
Allusions to that 'other life' of yours,
Though dropped obliquely as one might expect.

The 'friction', the 'rough ground' (or trade), the 'walk'
In Vienna's Prater that you often took
As Bartley told us in that scabrous book
Of his that prompted so much prurient talk –

Add 'slippery', and the passage then evokes,
As if by some associative chain
Of metonyms, the kinds of scene that pain
You now, brought back in memory's vivid strokes.

You'd not much time for Freud – you thought him clever,
Too clever for his own (or patients') good –
Maybe because he'd soon have understood
Your case and even recommended you should sever

Those ties, such as they were, that seemed to tear
Your soul apart between the smooth and rough,
The seminar-room in Cambridge where your stuff
Was too revered, or feared, to get its share

Of detailed criticism, and – so hard
To reconcile with that – your evening cruise
When the world changed to one where you could lose
Your Cambridge carapace and drop your guard.

Those mental notices, 'Keep off the ice',
'Life-hazard', 'watch your step', have set their seal
So deeply on your mindset that 'ideal',
The very word, seems often to suffice

For any notion, concept, or idea
In logic, physics or whatever field
Where counterfactual premises may yield
Good data after the corrective steer.


III


For it's in the rough ground you have your stake,
The ground of common practices, of maths
(The basics of arithmetic – no paths
To Gödel, Turing or, for pity's sake,

The set-theoretic paradoxes, zones
Of ice so hard and air so rarefied
That your spade turns and feet begin to slide
Like thoughts wrongfooted by unknown unknowns.

'Back to the rough ground' meant 'no losing touch
With numbers we can count on, language-games
In common use, and speculative claims
Trimmed tightly to the normal range of such

Familiar practices as take their lead
And working principles from what's the rule
Amongst practitioners who went to school
With teachers likewise – by and large – agreed.

That's where you looked for it, the needful friction
To get a foothold, never slide or slip,
Have no 'ideal conditions' ease your grip,
And deem their use in physics science-fiction.

Meanwhile, and altogether elsewhere, they,
Your Prater-bound sad captains, spare a thought
For him, 'the scary one, a brainy sort,
And father rich as Croesus, so they say,

Though he, young Ludwig, turned to academe,
Wrote famous books, was held by some a saint
For his ascetic life-style (well, he ain't,
As we can vouch!), and chose a work-regime

As fiercely single-minded in its quest
For truth as in the quest for love that drove
Him through the Prater's precincts as he strove
To lay desires, like fallacies, to rest'.

So they, old secret-sharers, now divine
From some chance recollection how close-kin
The two vocations are, how skin-to-skin
Encounters may in later life define

The thought-paths followed up and those eschewed
For reasons inaccessible except
At moments when some metaphor long kept
At bay reveals a detour long pursued.

# 35 Philosophy, language, music

*The silent adjustments to understand colloquial language
are enormously complicated.*

*I think I summed up my attitude to philosophy when I said:
philosophy ought really to be written only as a poetic
composition.*


I


A general point you're making here, of course:
The sheer amount of tinkering one must do
To fit, finagle, fettle, maybe force
Those formal structures on the *parlez-vous*
Of common language-use since they've their source
In logical constructions apt to slew
The sense so fluent speakers won't endorse
The regimen their speech is subject to.

Or then again, the point may be to stress
How hard it is, how many system-tweaks
Are needed, if the habits of address
That typically show up when someone speaks
Familiarly to someone else can mess
Quite badly with the formalised techniques
That linguists use and have them acquiesce
In sundry add-ons till the framework creaks.

Or, nearer home: might not the passage bear
A hint of just how badly ill-at-ease
You felt in company, how self-aware
In party-talk, and how intent to seize
On any English idiom to repair
The expressive deficit whose indices
Each begged an extra tweak whereby to share
The language-game that let them shoot the breeze?

Then might not your discomfiture connote,
To readers well-attuned, your introvert
Amazement that those others should devote
Themselves to social chat and bet their shirt
On getting through, or keeping – just – afloat,
And neither suffering nor inflicting hurt
As evidenced in many an anecdote
That shows what dark-side powers you could exert.

## II

'Charisma': not a term one might expect,
Or wish, to find too frequently applied
To serious thinkers – Socrates, hen-pecked
Made fun of, threatened, often vilified
Is more the mark. Yet you've your loyal sect,
Albeit disputatious, still bug-eyed,
With some whose pride or confidence you wrecked
And who still claim to see your saintly side.

The charismatic in you left the saint
With mounting credibility arrears
As things came out that left, let's say, a taint
Of less-than-saintly conduct, like the years
In Otterthal when he lay in a faint,
That child you beat, as if his cries and tears
Drove you to block all promptings of restraint,
Like one possessed until the red mist clears.

This leaves 'charisma' as the favoured match
Since better placed to gauge the depth of your
Unfathomed contrarieties and catch
Some lingering echoes from the ocean floor
Of what strange fascinations might attach
To that same quality that seems to draw
Rapt devotees like ephebes keen to snatch
The parabolic gist they're yearning for.

You said 'best give it up, that vain pursuit,
But if you really must philosophise
Then let it be in poetry' – astute,
That comment, since it's often given rise
To lit-crit stratagems that would recruit
Your cherished texts and thus bring fresh supplies
Of your charisma back to help reboot
Their these days somewhat jaded enterprise.

# III

Poetry, not verse, you said, and so
Let on that it was German works you had
Specifically in mind, the kind we know
As *Hochromantik* since they'd have us glad
To feel, not think too clearly, and forego
Those remnant prosy virtues – syntax-clad,
Thought-bearing, apt to say as much as show –
That might too quickly stop one going mad.

What you're obliquely telling us in that
Much puzzled-over saying is that we've
Gone wrong – not figured what you're aiming at –
If we think you've the answers up your sleeve
And need just don your sorter-outer's hat
To have those error-prone personae leave
The page and reason's dicta end the spat
With poetry denied one more reprieve.

No, you've much bigger fish to fry, and it's
Where poetry and charisma share the stage
That their joint leverage skews the working fits
Whereby, since Plato, reason could engage
The passions, and those passions try their wits
In reason's court, then both consent to wage
An agon where no party rightly sits
In judgment through such sneaky arbitrage.

You've tweaked the rules and offered them a *don*
*Du poème*, those philosophers, that they
Seem oddly predisposed to fasten on,
A psychomachic language-game to play
When their more customary lexicon
Falls silent, not in the *Tractatus* way
Of folding up when logic's props have gone,
But switching modes so *Dichtung* has its say.

And so it is that your chief aim – to coax
Them down from high-flown talk so they'd make sense
In language shared with ordinary folks –
Bears unexpected fruit when they commence
A depth-charged eisegesis that evokes
The psychic needs they'd have you recompense
Poetically, or by those sudden strokes
Of metaphor where hopes and fears condense.

# 36 Life, death, timelessness – and Hell!

*Hell isn't other people. Hell is yourself.*

*Death is not an event of life. Death is not lived through.*

*If by eternity is understood not endless temporal duration
but timelessness, then he lives eternally who lives in the
present. Our life is endless in the way that our visual field
is without limit.*

Hell isn't other people; hell
Is you yourself, so just tell Sartre:
Such thoughts make headlines in Montmartre
But here they don't go down so well.

It's basically just one long whinge,
His 'existentialist' *j'accuse*.
Why let those other folk impinge?
They're worlds apart, so just refuse!

Granted, it's hell enough to be
Shut up with no one but myself
And that deictic pronoun, 'me',
To tell them: 'poor chap, on the shelf'.

Yet it's not solipsism, my
(As they'd say) 'otherworldly' state
Of mind, but the whole world that I,
Its focal centre, contemplate.

So, too, with 'other people', those,
The talking ones, who occupy
My visual field until life's close –
My life, of course, since who'd deny

That their existence can't extend
Beyond the life-horizon that
Assigns the time-span due to end
Whenever I hang up my hat.

I made it clear: take your last breath
And a world ceases but you'll not
Experience it, the point of death,
Since life-time's all the time you've got.

They say 'of course he's what they call
Autistic, that chap Wittgenstein,
Cut off, not up to all that small-
Talk stuff – those downcast eyes, sure sign!'.

I say: yes, would be hell if they,
The party-goers and the slaves
Of 'common-sense', just had their way
And broke the peace my spirit craves.

But if the question's put so starkly
I'll opt for Pascal's empty spaces,
Take sides (perforce) with Bishop Berkeley,
And face them down, those party-faces.

# 37 Death, insanity, and 'taking for granted'

*You must always be puzzled by mental illness. The thing I would dread most, if I became mentally ill, would be your adopting a common-sense attitude; that you could take it for granted that I was deluded.*

*Freud's idea: in madness the lock is not destroyed, only altered; the old key can no longer unlock it, but it could still be opened by a differently constructed key.*

I

It's your accepting it that I most dread,
Your crediting so quickly that I've lost
My wits, or paid at last the heavy cost
Of all that time I spent inside my head.

You'd quickly take for granted that I'm mad
Because, presumably, you'd always thought
Me, Ludwig, manifestly just the sort
To have them looking for a cell to pad.

And, truth to tell, I've no right to complain
If, knowing me so well, you've then concluded
'Poor Wittgenstein, he's certainly deluded,
If not – so cruel to speak the word! – insane'.

For I've long entertained the thought and feared,
Not without reason, that ere long I'd be
Quite without reason when it rendered me,
By Act 3, Scene 2 (so to speak) King-Leared.

## II

I tend to blame it on their 'attitude',
Their treating me as if mere common-sense
Required they reconstrue past evidence
In light of 'all the signs' lately accrued.

'O let me not be mad', he cries, and shows,
By that same plea, how readily the mind,
Or some small part of it, may come to find
Its fears predestining the way it goes.

Small wonder if that's just the way they're slanted,
Those anxious questions charitably meant
Yet sure to make me ask myself: what went
To have their covert point taken for granted?

So let the puzzlement be yours and mine,
Our joint defence against the terror-numbed,
Unpuzzled reflex that's too soon succumbed
To that would-be apotropaic line.

## III

Be sure, it's not my 'case' alone that's here
In question – not the mind-state, sane or crazed,
Of Ludwig Wittgenstein – but the case raised
For mortal souls whose essence must inhere

In that which constitutes them, each alone,
An entity, a substance, that choice pick
Of conjoint traits that soul's arithmetic
Computes the sum of those to call its own.

Russell may scoff, but then, what term but 'soul'
Can offer all the scholiasts provide
To make good what he chooses to deride? –
An image of rent psyche rendered whole.

It's this they take away, those who'd deprive
The mad, the half-mad, or mad Nor'-Nor'-West,
When they next face the dinner-party test,
Of what might just allow them to survive.


IV

The wounded psyche craves what they'd forfend,
Its cleavage healed, its hope of hopes renewed
Beyond whatever mental harms ensued
Once some short-lived remission had an end.

The psyche-doctor plies his useful trade,
Brings temporary salves, but must concede
His talking cure will service every need
Except the need for soul to come in aid.

None wiser, shrewder than Professor Freud
For such disturbances in psyche's realm,
Yet nothing they'll so quickly overwhelm
As those soul-famished techniques he deployed.

Like Hamlet, I've a sense that madness lurks
Somewhere offstage and, at odd moments, casts
A shadow of insanity that lasts
Till thoughts of soul resume their healing work.

102

# V

'Just wishful thinking', Russell says: 'no use
Pretending "let's pretend" can make it so.'
I take his point, but let the challenge go –
My need, his lucid reasoning: no excuse!

And yet, and yet: why think the language-game
Of soul should, any more than that of prayer,
Yield place to his decree and bring despair
To lives reliant on that counter-claim?

For what if soul alone should satisfy
The need for that which succours and subtends
The psyche, or on which the mind depends
When words go missing, errors multiply,

A stray thought calls in doubt all you've achieved
To keep stray thoughts in check, and nothing holds
It back, the creeping chaos that enfolds
The self unsouled, unselved, unself-deceived.

# 38 Philosophy, scribbles, and 'what's that?'

*Philosophers often behave like little children who scribble some marks on a piece of paper at random and then ask the grown-up "What's that?" – It happened like this: the grown-up had drawn pictures for the child several times and said: this is a man, this is a house, etc. And then the child makes some marks too and asks: what's this then?"*

I

Unless the child should ask 'Please, will you draw
[Let's say] a princess?', and you try your best,
Ineptly, to get through this simple test
With dignity intact, and she says 'Aw,

What's that then, Daddy?', and – the final straw –
Proceeds to draw a princess, finely dressed
But oddly skewed as if to manifest
Both her superior skill and, too, the flaw

Of reasoning that made you think she saw
No more to drawing than some arid quest
For what she did with ease yet then finessed
By slight infractions of Alberti's law.

No getting back to likeness in the raw,
But then, let's not have parents too distressed
By subtler changes made at the behest
Of promptings alien to Maw and Paw.

## II

You made your mark by making marks that we,
Your readers, figure out as best we can
Yet never know quite how to read or scan
Since apt, like Daddy, to suppose the key

Comes with an adult willingness to see
'As a child sees' but play Renaissance man
And think it's where art-history began,
Along with that odd trick of commentary

On Wittgenstein where there's a special plea
For thoughts that often seem more childlike than
The adult norm. They leave those also-ran
Art-critics, Wittgensteinians, and would-be

Child-friendly furnishers of fatherly
Instruction to adapt their master-plan
And not stand too securely in the van
When who knows who's next up to bend the knee?

## III

It happened like this: you'd have us suppose
A child quite unfamiliar, as yet,
With what it means to 'draw', or find she's met,
Or failed to meet, the standards for what goes

To make a proper 'drawing' of all those
Assorted swirls and squiggles that she's set
Before you, she who simply doesn't *get*
The 'form of life' in question – and it shows!

What's more, when reading you the feeling grows,
At times, that you're, like her, inclined to fret
At ways of making sense that pose a threat
To you at first because they seem to close

You off from something everybody knows
But you, some world where other kids' *vignettes*
Win praise but, in your case, the mild regret
That yours can't be the one your teacher chose.


IV

What brings her out in you, that 'child within'? –
Bewildered, not at home with how they speak,
Those others; how they seem to form a clique
Of language-gamers distantly akin

To how you talk, and draw, and put your spin
On their strange words, but always by oblique
Or noisy channels where the signal's weak
And all it lets you do is try to pin

The odd phrase down. Then, maybe, you'll begin –
Like her, the squiggle-picture child – to seek
Whatever helps sustain that *Midrashic*
Of yours, that art of somehow finding in

Such occult utterances a means to win
The rapt devotion of all those who pique
Themselves on having tapped the Hoffmann streak
Of deep-laid fears far back in origin.

# 39 Inner process, outward criteria

*An inner process stands in need of outward criteria . . . .*

. . . or so it did in your case, so it did
In the extreme yet self-revealing case
Of one who so conspicuously 'hid

Himself away', assumed no public face,
And opted early on to place a lid
Of privacy on any 'inner space'

Where psycho-sleuths might delve and make their bid
For some fresh invitation to the chase.
Yet if the serious commentary soon slid

Into a vulgar-Freudian database
For those who'd make your conflict-ridden id
Their happy hunting ground, why then that race

To trawl the turbid depths that quite undid
Your rule that they remain a private place
Since, like deep-sea disturbances amid

Calm waters, it's the tell-tale surface trace
That counts. Then all your strategies to rid
Our minds of Private Ludwig won't efface

The evidence of your desire to rid
The outer self, if not that 'inner space',
Of what instilled the lifelong need to kid
Yourself as demon fears crept on apace.

# 40 Ideas before they are ripe

*Ideas too sometimes fall from the tree before they are ripe .*
*. .*

## I

. . . or so I tell myself: that all I say
Must strike them, Bertie and the rest, as fruit
So strange, so sour at times, so destitute
Of Summer warmth and wholesomeness that they

Suspect – and who can blame them? – some decay
Or soul-infecting canker at the root
And frame their pet hypotheses to suit
My low-grade produce, such as might convey

Their sense of something in me knocked astray
By upbringing, inheritance, acute
And morbid sensitivity, or loot
(That family fortune made the shadiest way!),

Or 'old Vienna' and its cabaret
Of decadence and vices they'd impute –
Again, with justice – to this feeble shoot
Of an old tree that might put out a spray

Of faded blossoms yearly to delay
The final chop but lacks that attribute
Of mellow fruitfulness in whose pursuit
My Cambridge fellows pick their crop each day.

## II

And yet, I sometimes wonder: why construe
That Lear-inflected self-report of mine
As if intended simply to malign
My under-ripeness, simply have it do

Their work, those second-rate Russellians who,
Like him, pass up on no chance to opine
Concerning 'that pure genius, Wittgenstein',
Though then – like him again, I fear – review

Their commendation every time some new
Remark I make has them once more consign
Me to the category of superfine
But unripe intellects that somehow grew,

As if by inter-breeding, quite askew
From common sense and logic. Why decline
What he, my kindlier angel, might divine:
The sense of 'ripe' that has them, Russell's crew,

Too much mere creatures of their time, or too
*Echt*-Cambridge, not to join the chorus-line
Of those who much preferred the anodyne
Appeal of present-best *idées reçues*,

And therefore 'bit off more than they could chew',
As that lot say, since apt to pluck the vine
Of fruits whose future worth, like laid-up wine,
Must wait till their acknowledgment falls due.

# 41 Small thought to fill a life . . . .

'How small a thought it takes to fill a life.'
Perhaps the life was hollowed out by thought
Whose elbow-room it is, your life in small.

Such well-turned phrases for such mental strife!
'Great reck'nings in a little room' you sought,
Each framed just so, as if to say: close call!

Life-forms mutate, false language-games are rife;
Stay sane, cut verbiage, keep the syntax taut!
The forms and games yet multiply withal.

Change Ockham's Razor for the paring knife;
Count nonsense-talk a pleasure dearly bought
For all its power to baffle and enthral.
'How small a thought it takes to fill a life.'

# 42 Face, body, soul

*The face is the soul of the body.*

Your poet-prophet knew whereof he spake:
'The lineaments of satisfied desire';
Soul's body, body's soul – the human face.

Yet those there are who'd ask of William Blake:
'How then shall we, the unsatisfied, aspire
To such ensoulment or obtain such grace?

Grant us our little share, for pity's sake,
When next you so insistently enquire
What joys, what fears, what horrors left their trace

On these drawn lineaments, or what could make
Of those now famous photographs so dire
A chronicle of ills on which to base

A shrink's report. If war once failed to break
My trait of heedless courage under fire,
Then what's to say when it becomes a case

Of all the inward turns that mood may take
When thought's incessant psychic costs run higher
Than anything your poet Blake may place

In Urizen's domain, or where the stake
Is such as bids the canny shrink: retire,
Leave ill enough alone, vacate this space!

# 43 Ethics and Aesthetics are one.

Your thought: both are conceived *sub specie*
*Aeternitatis*, not at all as we're
Accustomed to have deeds and things appear
When met with in the course of everyday

Experience, but as singled out to play
A role that could or should transcend the sphere
Of purposive cognition or of mere
Self-interest. Thus they'd set us on the way

To that which you, like Schopenhauer, portray
As the best means to lift ourselves quite clear
Of all those base attachments that adhere
To acts and objects brought beneath the sway

Of calculative reason. That might pay
Us off in terms of benefits held dear,
Or profit, or what's thought to interfere
With that blest state of mind in which they pray,

The faithful, that no impure thought betray
How suchlike worldly motives come to rear
Their ugly heads. They'd strip the thin veneer
Of contemplation from its underlay

Of motives, drives, desires, and all that they,
Aesthetes and ethicists, consider sheer
Backsliding and a proof that such austere
Demands must always send some folk astray

Since framed precisely – *vide* Kant – to say:
'Abandon hope, all ye who enter here,
If not prepared, when called upon, to jeer
At those who'll let some *Lustprinzip* defray

The cost of keeping profit-thoughts away
By having pleasure-guards pace the frontier
Where ethics and aesthetics tend to veer
Into a self-willed state of disarray'.

Yet Ludwig, might they not, those feet of clay,
Belong to high-toned moralists who sneer
From their well-insulated social tier
At any complications apt to weigh

More heavily with those condemned to play
The plaintiff role, or aesthetes whose career
As (say) art-critic or art-auctioneer
Dictates they keep such scruples well at bay.

Best think eternity's another day,
Treat art and morals firmly in the here-
And-now of mortal lives and, peer-to-peer,
Adjudicate their claims as best we may

While seeing how, for you who'd kicked away
So many ladders, simply shifting gear
To an atemporal zone might help to clear
Your mind of a more grievous *temps passé*.

# 44 No surprises in logic

*There can never be surprises in logic.*

*When I came home I expected a surprise and there was no surprise for me, so of course I was surprised.*

*More wisdom is contained in the best crime fiction than in philosophy.*


To know what follows logically from what
Won't rock your boat by springing huge surprises,
Though switching terms and functions, slot-to-slot,
May generate some pretty wild surmises.

It's there in every good detective plot
When some new twist of story-line arises
And logic's light brigade are quick to spot
Whatever tricks the novelist devises.

That's why I think detective fiction's got
The edge: each plot-development revises
Our grasp of what's now valid and what's not
As clues accrue and Marlowe realises

That up to now, goddammit, he's been hot
On the wrong trail; then quickly criticises
His own flawed reasoning, and has a shot
At some new telling of it that comprises

All the known facts along with quite a lot
Of known unknowns but handily downsizes
The unknown unknowns so the logic-knot
Pulls tighter with each twist he analyses.

Myself, I liked surprises as a tot,
Looked forward to them, though what exercises
My adult mind is how, when they forgot
To lay one on, it caused a minor crisis

As I thought, sadly: what's surprising's what
Turns out to be the absence of surprises
When one's expected, and precisely not
The turn-up every chancer fantasises.

# 45 Only describe, don't explain

*Belief in the causal nexus is superstition.*

*I am aiming at something different than are the scientists*
*and my thoughts move differently than do theirs.*

*Man has to awaken to wonder – and so perhaps do*
*peoples. Science is a way of sending him to sleep again.*
*Philosophy limits the disputable sphere of natural science.*

I

You tell us 'just describe, please don't explain',
As if a chief witch-doctor told his tribe:
'You've done no dancing and there's been no rain;
What more's to say? It's just as I describe!'.

If you weren't anti-science you'd refrain
From offering them such potions to imbibe,
Unless you thought they couldn't stand the strain
Of coming off that trance-inducing vibe.

Then you might join the dance and not disdain
To offer him, the Sun-God, the one bribe
That's guaranteed to lift the annual bane
Of drought and risk no science-fancier's gibe.

## II

But then, you'd not much time for talk of cause-
Effect, of warm fronts, cold fronts, or indeed
Of drought so far as that might conjure laws
Of nature and suggest the tribe would need

At least some opportune exemption-clause
To let them drop the hallowed rain-dance creed
When it stays dry, or put the thing on pause
Lest some drought-friendly god should intercede.

It's odd, that anti-science thing of yours,
The thing that has you much prefer to heed
Some ritual, cult, or rigmarole that draws
On god knows what dark sources to mislead

Your fideist tribe and have them clutch at straws
That show how superstitions may yet breed
In minds disposed to treat the slightest flaws
In science as proof it has no case to plead.


## III

Odd, too, that you should think it a prime role
That any good philosopher must fill
To 'limit' natural science, or control

Whatever deep-laid drive it has to spill
Across its proper bounds and take for goal
The public obligation to instil

A due respect for science as our sole
Defence against – what else? – the kind of skill
You have with those deep sayings that cajole

Devoted readers to affirm they will,
On your advice, head down the rabbit-hole
And get by heart the who-needs-science drill.


IV

The science thing, the maths thing, and the thing
With engineering – gave them your best try
But all the experts soon contrived to bring
The lesson home: no way that you'd get by

On their terrain except as one more fling
At doing something that would satisfy
Your need to break their hold, those fears that cling
To every waking thought, those thoughts that lie

(Yet how?) 'too deep for words', those words that spring
Perplexities you struggle to deny,
And every mental screw whose tightening
Exerts new pressures you alone apply.


V

Strikes me that maths and science helped you swing
Your mind elsewhere, have novel thoughts defy
Old thought-routines, and salve the conscience-sting
You felt 'beneath the great task-master's eye'.

It seemed to you the sciences might ring
More truly to your avocation, vie
More strongly with philosophy to string
Your febrile thoughts together and, thereby,

Provide fresh means for soul's refurbishing.
Yet somehow your best efforts went awry,
Especially your patent rotary-wing
Machine with jet-powered rotor-tips whose high-

Stress liabilities outran the zing
Of pure invention so it wouldn't fly,
The idea or the craft, and patenting
An unproved concept rather wiped your eye.


VI


Gödel and Turing, too, chose to make known
That it was no high estimate they set
On your maths notions, like the Cantor-bone
You picked (thus: how could finite reckoners get

On terms with infinites and such high-flown
Abstractions?), or your tendency to fret
At those, like Turing, whose ideas you'd shown –
By your occluding lights – not to have met

The test of sticking firmly to the zone
Of language-games perceived to pose no threat
To shared thought-practices in which we'd grown
Up long enough to own no other debt.

Let's not say 'scientific cover blown',
But rather: 'what's the real cause for regret
Is how your later efforts to atone
For early failures led you to abet

Those anti-science trends that they're so prone,
Your followers, to take on board and let
Such empty talk of science as a (groan!)
Cultural 'form of life' become the pet

Idea of those who, once the seed's been sown,
Turn what were live debating-points as yet
Into a creed those prelates might condone
Whose instruments had Galileo sweat.

# 46 Language, imagination, forms of life

*To imagine a language is to imagine a form of life.*

### I

Ah yes, but Ludwig, just think, just suppose,
Or (just my point!) imagine how they teem,
Those life-forms, how unstoppable the flows
Of sheer inventiveness, how any theme,

Though well-worn, might give access to who knows
What timely tappings of what fecund seam
Till now unvisited, and thus disclose
Not only problems with some in-place scheme

Of thought but an alternative that goes
So far toward truth's ever-distant gleam
That any spanner its arrival throws
Into the language-works we'd likely deem

Not just a novel move but one of those
Game-changers, as they'd find, the soccer team
Whose flagrant handball, when the whistle blows,
Creates a whole new game and rule-regime.

### II

No doubt you'll say: 'ah, but that 'whole new game'
You confidently speak of must presume
A whole array of rules that stay the same
Across such changes while still leaving room

For all the fine inventiveness you claim
Must, on occasion, brandish a new broom,
Then feel its bristles strong enough to tame
Old customs, have a thousand new flowers bloom,

Yet still, like hot-house plants, require some frame
Of cultural sustenance although you plume
Yourselves on how, Simplicius-like, you came
To take the leap no custom could subsume'.

### III

But Ludwig, when you put your case – and yes,
It's true up to a point – why take as your
Exemplar, or the analogue you stress
Above all else, the natural-language store

Of speech-forms, idioms, phrases to express
The run of human feelings (metaphor
At hand where needed), and the more-or-less
Communicable language-games we shore

Against our fears of solitude? They press
On you, self-islanded, with all the more
Tormenting force for the contrariness
With which you drive well-wishers from your door

While longed-for speech-communities redress,
In thought at least, that lost *esprit de corps*
Whose saving bond of amity might bless
With fitting words your intra-psychic war.

## IV

And yet, I ask: why should they acquiesce,
Your exegetes, in being washed ashore
Like clueless Crusoes, fated to regress
Beyond all shared horizons and implore

Salvation from whatever thoughts possess
The spell to fake it, like your wishful lore
Of language-games and life-forms that confess,
By making custom king, how they ignore

Those disciplines of thought where such excess
Authority as natural language bore
For you would soon see science obsolesce,
With mathematics, to a stage before

Abstraction, logic and their accentless
Yet myth-dispelling concepts let us draw
Far-reaching thoughts that cosy knowingness
Would have us shun in superstitious awe.

# 47 Don't think, but look

*The problems are solved, not by giving new information,*
*but by re-arranging what we have known for a long time.*

How odd you'd have us make that choice between
(Say) 'look and think', or 'look, don't think, just leap'.
The vacant gaze perceives no vivid scene.

The tensed grasshopper's leaps are quick and clean,
All tricky landings conjured at a peep.
How odd you'd have us make that choice between.

Of course it's 'seeing-as' you really mean,
Duck/rabbit, switching aspects half-asleep.
The vacant gaze perceives no vivid scene.

But Socrates – the grasshopper – could glean
What's vital through thought-motions quick though deep;
How odd you'd have us make that choice between.

Ours to arrange thoughts lucidly and wean
Ourselves off thoughts that just won't earn their keep.
The vacant gaze perceives no vivid scene.

Think rather: thought *and* vision must be keen
Should cost and rate of climb not grow too steep.
How odd you'd have us make that choice between;
The vacant gaze perceives no vivid scene.

# 48 Erecting walls in philosophy

*The aim of philosophy is to erect a wall at the point where language stops anyway.*

Why, then, a wall if that's where language ends?
What use if words run out with no way through?
Whence your desire for this redundant wall?

As if writ large on it, the word it sends
Is Kafka's Gatekeeper's: 'Meant just for you,
This obstacle with its Belshazzar scrawl'.

Conceive no language-game whose scope extends
Beyond what natives readily construe
Lest into nonsense it should quickly fall.

Yet on such nonsense frequently depends,
Rosetta-like, the sudden *aperçu*
That conjures up what long seemed past recall.

It's the wall-builder in you apprehends
The shock of language-vistas glimpsed anew
From deep within the life-form they befall.

For you, no *vita nuova* makes amends
For all that's lost in such a forced review
Of *vita ante acta* and of all

That once held out against linguistic trends
Whose innovations must at length accrue
As woods and fields yield ground to urban sprawl.

# 49 Off the beaten track

*A good guide will take you through the more important*
*streets more often than he leads you down side-streets; a*
*bad guide will do the opposite. In philosophy I'm a rather*
*bad guide.*

False modesty, of course – with you as guide
We get to see some pretty classy streets
And parts of town, though yes, you do take pride
In showing us 'the muttering retreats'

Of Eliot's seedy precincts and provide
A sense of the vast labyrinth that greets
The back-street walker as his bearings slide
And a brief glimpse of some far boulevard meets

His questing gaze, then leaves him swivel-eyed
And wondering what new red-light district treats
Might be in store. Talk of the 'seamy side'
And your late-nightly Prater-cruising beats

Those fluttered scholar-dovecotes, yet why hide
What rumours hit the prurient tabloid sheets
And then, once taken gradually in stride
By devotees, illumined those conceits

Of yours where it's the traveller's aid supplied
By low-life types or savvy logothetes
That sees you through and not the bona fide
Tour-managers or scholarly elites.

For that's where your back-alley scouts are spied
Updating notes, and where keen ear defeats
Sharp eye as the modality best tried
In those dark quarters where the ringside seats

Are had by those, like you, who may reside
Uptown but know the ropes, like cockney Keats,
And take a walk – in your case, short tram-ride –
To visit those multiloquent mean streets.

# 50 Scientists, poets, musicians

*People nowadays think that scientists exist to instruct*
*them, poets, musicians, etc. to give them pleasure. The*
*idea that these have something to teach them – that does*
*not occur to them.*

I Haydn

What do I learn from Haydn? That quick wit,
Good humour, equability, and rare
Fool-tolerance, not qualities I share,
Are very likely those most requisite

For living long, making the best of it
When marriage sours, musicians' tempers flare,
Court hangers-on just want their standard fare,
And then Prince Esterhazy makes you sit

Around all Summer for an extra bit
Of entertainment. Why should genius bear
Such slights, I ask myself, when I despair
Of every human folly, think to quit

My Cambridge friends and colleagues as unfit
For my exalted company, and care
As much for my small errors as for their
Long-feared descent to depths they'd scarce admit.

Haydn it was who raised me from the pit
Of endless, vain self-catechising where
I'd licked my wounds into the larger air
Of Tyrol, birdsong-bright and leafmeal-lit,

The air he breathed but I must counterfeit
As best I may by trying, if I dare,
To have my violent mood-swings somehow square
With his key-shifts, deep-felt yet exquisite.

II Schubert

What do I learn from Schubert? That one mark
Of genius is the courage to offset
Lost loves, grief, pain, the all-encroaching dark
Of early death foreknown against your debt

To music, to its being there, the ark
Of some last-movement promise, or the net
That's still in place when tidings are too stark
And only music can avert a threat

So great that I, a strict close-listener, park
My principles and, *pace* Hanslick, let
My knowledge of his life have me embark
On his sublime C Major String Quintet.


III Brahms

What do I learn from Brahms? Well, to begin:
That need of ours, 'us Germans', to have soul
Not take depth-plumbing as the only role
That we should see as fit to glory in.

His Trio, say – horn, piano, violin –
The second-movement scherzo almost droll
Or frolicsome though, taken as a whole,
The work conveys how hard it was to win

That brief reprieve from all that churned within
The soul of one whose 'Lullaby' once stole
On countless ears and tells how great a toll
It took, the mother's death and origin

Of this Horn Trio. 'Show you're Brahms's kin',
My conscience says, 'let humour seize control
From gravitas once in a while and bowl
The listener over with a timely spin

On Nietzsche's rants against the *echt-Deutsch* sin
Of excess soulfulness. Then a short stroll
Or breath of mountain air should soon cajole
The brooding *Übermensch* out of his skin.


IV


'Ludwig, please lighten up for just a while',
Folk say to me, as no doubt once they bent
His ear, the glum Johannes, and so went
The wrong way round if hoping to beguile

That unrevealing countenance to 'smile
Despite the tears', or that dark temperament
To have its inner censorship relent
And those contending forces reconcile.

Much better had they not said 'Please don't pile
The agony on', or told you to 'accent
The positive', but brought the strength they lent,
My friends who urged that I not so revile

Myself for sins – no-one more versatile
As self-inquisitor! – which I'd frequent
In guilt-filled dreams and strivings to repent
Each entry in my bulging conscience-file.

Then, Johannes, they'd not so much make trial
Of your scant patience nor regret time spent
In vain but, like those friends of mine, content
Themselves to note that scherzo's buoyant style.


V


That's what I learn from Brahms: his knowing how
To have some change of pulse or key-shift raise
His spirits even on the darkest days
And thereby, as if magically, allow

The attentive listener likewise to endow
A passage, melody, or transient phrase
With power to end that melancholy phase
So that its presence in the here-and-now

Of lived experience has them quietly vow,
As I do when some formulation plays
A kindred role, to see that it conveys
To others what once cleared a darkened brow.

# 51 Philosophy, learning, recollection

*Learning philosophy is really recollecting. We remember that we really used words in this way.*

I

But did we, Ludwig, did we really use
Those same words 'the same way' last year, last week,
Or just a moment back? Or might we speak
Them now and ask some phonetician whose

Trained ear we trust to soundly disabuse
Us of such hyperbolic doubts, or seek
A linguist who'll soon check us for some freak
Of deviant usage, or, perhaps, accuse

Ourselves of just not knowing when we lose
The sense-conserving thread? Then meanings leak,
Words sicken, and it might be ancient Greek
We're speaking to ourselves for all the clues

That memory yields when sceptics put the screws
On all we think we know and, from that bleak
Surmise, go on to demonstrate how weak
The best, the sturdiest strategies we choose,

When thus provoked, to don the sceptic's shoes,
Think just like them, and so, by such oblique
Assay, conduct a brisk auto-critique
And have plain commonsense exact its dues.

## II

But Ludwig, take a look, see all those flies
Still buzzing round the fly-bottle you guessed –
Mistakenly, it seems – they'd do their best
To get well clear of once they recognise

Your good intent. You'd have them realise
How scepticism always fails the test,
The one you so insistently addressed
By showing firstly that it self-applies,

Thus self-refutes, and second – no surprise,
Given how long and deeply you obsessed
Over that issue – that what's manifest
To commonsense may nonetheless disguise

Deep sources of disquiet whose rumbling tries
The nerve and patience even of those blest,
Like you, with great resources to invest
In risking such opaque words to the wise.

## III

For that's the bitterest irony that lies
Behind your running claim to have finessed
The sceptic's strongest points: that it confessed,
At every stage, how intricate the ties

Between your sense-restoring enterprise
And the increasing subtlety and zest
With which they so meticulously pressed
Their case for giving you the booby-prize

Since you yourself seem fated to capsize
That leaky boat whenever they suggest
Some further patch-up. Else you keep abreast
Of theirs by some manoeuvre that just buys

You time enough to fix or improvise
A comeback strategy. This they'll digest
And use, or so re-fashion, cards to chest,
That yours seems a beginner's exercise.


IV

'Only as poetry': that's how you told
The faithful they should 'do philosophy',
Perhaps through some such sharp dichotomy –
One the Tractarian Ludwig would uphold –

Between those strictly ordered thoughts that mould
Themselves to the inflexible decree
Of superordinate necessity,
And, all around, a border-zone patrolled

On both sides by strict arbiters enrolled
To keep apart what's properly to be
Accounted part of logic's territory
And what won't let itself be pigeonholed

Or brought within that ordered manifold
By way of propositions since the key
Is how the bounds of say-ability
Are, for you, those of poetry's threshold.

## V

But no: when you say poetry's the mode
In which philosophy should best be done,
It's not *Tractatus*-ward our thoughts should run,
But more toward the change of heart that flowed

From your mid-life decision to offload
That creaky structure you'd now have us shun
And dwell within the web of words you'd spun.
This we could make our everyday abode,

We flies unbottled, yet with every node
Of that wing-binding web most likely one
That's just so placed as to ensure that none
Of our buzz-words is artfully bestowed

And might thereby disturb the language-code
That marks such deviations from the run
Of common usage with the caution: 'un-
Received, unnatural, like a midwife toad!'.

## VI

One thing's for sure: my verses wouldn't have gained
A kindly hearing from the man whose 'taste
In poetry' (ridiculous phrase!) embraced
The German high-Romantic line and deigned

To give no work that title which profaned
The transcendental valuation placed
On symbol, metaphor, and all that faced
Away from time and change. Such poems strained

To somehow capture that 'white radiance' stained
By a 'dome of many-coloured glass' still based,
As Shelley says, on earthly ground and cased
Around by whatsoever yet remained

Of mortal sensibilities that craned
Within the dome for mystic figures traced
In a symbolic language that effaced
All signs of how that state might be attained.


## VII

That's why I say you'd find my verse a slur
On 'poetry', that cryptic over-flyer
Of all that, post-*Tractatus*, you'd aspire
To put behind you, all that you'd refer

To Russell's cast-off influence and deter
The faithful from pursuing since they'd tire,
Like you, of logic's striving to acquire
Such wisdom as demands they should concur

With how you see things now. Thus you'd demur
At my still dragging readers through the mire
Of concepts, propositions, that entire
(You'd have it) catalogue of ways to err

When doing philosophy, and have them blur
The line between it and poetry to fire
Them up with thoughts less likely to expire
For lack of metaphor's creative spur.

# VIII

I say, conversely: Ludwig, if you sought
To make philosophy more 'poetic', you'd
Perhaps have done much better to include
In 'poetry' such verse-forms as they wrought

Who deemed it fitting that a line of thought,
An argument, a thesis be pursued,
And propositional content not subdued
To symbol's ways of cutting reason short

By sovereign right. Poetic utterance ought,
By your lights, to present itself as food
For thought but only should the thinker's mood
Be one of contemplation, or the sort

Of rapt involvement reasoning won't distort
Since free of the hubristic attitude
You find in Frazer, Russell and their brood.
This recognises no such higher court

Since poems have no such calling to abort
The claim of reason, much less to collude
With language-games whose mind-set, thus renewed,
Might undo all the lessons reason brought.

'A versifier's credo', you'll retort,
'With *logos* always waiting to intrude'.
'Just a late stage', I say, 'in that old feud
That Plato sparked and poets overbought'.

## IX

For, Ludwig, it's a step too far to state
The case so flatly, with so little sign
Of needing – or of caring – to define
Just what you mean, that subsequent debate

Has largely been content to alternate
Between attempts to populate a line
Of Austro-German poets you'd incline,
On what small evidence we have, to rate

Amongst the fittest kinds of candidate,
And tired attempts to find some anodyne
Or fudgy way of having them combine,
Those ancient rivals, in an inchoate

But vaguely inspirational update
On *Leitmotifs* from Hölderlin's 'The Rhine',
From Rilke, and whatever they can mine
From Heidegger in full prophetic spate.

## X

Simply to turn the Plato charge straight back
Against the Platonists is to invite
Yet further struggles on the dizzying height
Of issues magnified the more for lack

Of intellectual substance. If they smack
Of oft-rewarmed old chestnuts, this just might
Be on account of one thing he got right,
That ancient Greek who managed so to stack

The odds that they, the poets he'd attack,
Were all conceived as rhapsodes in whose flight
Of *Schwärmerei* soul lost the oversight
Of mind and nothing else took up the slack

But mind's poor substitute, the huckster's knack
Of high-toned prophecy. So, when you write
That all philosophers should see the light
And don the poet's vatic robe, you shack

Up not exclusively with the A-pack
Of German poets but, as well, with quite
A varied bunch of mystagogues who might
More aptly star in Old Moore's Almanac.


## XI

Forgive me, then, dear Ludwig, for this show
Of nerve, or folly, or crass overreach
In having my verse-practice serve at each
Point as a stalking-horse for some low blow,

As it must seem, delivered *à propos*
A topic long dishonoured in the breach
Of good relations mourned by those who'd preach
That poets and philosophers forego

Such wrangling, sink their differences, and know –
As Plato's metaphors and similes teach
The attentive reader – how both sides beseech
We not once more let sounds of discord grow.

# 52 Inquisitor – 'the physiognomy of error'

*One of the most important tasks is to express all false
thought processes so characteristically that the reader
says, 'Yes, that's exactly the way I meant it'. To make a
tracing of the physiognomy of every error. Indeed, we can
only convict someone else of a mistake if he acknowledges
that this is the expression of his feeling.*

Forgive me, Ludwig, but this somewhat smacks
Of the inquisitor whose craving, keen
As his choice instruments, requires you mean
Just what you say – get right down to brass tacks!

No time for those whose language-games grow lax
Through failure to conceive what new machine
For lie-detection masks behind that screen
With nonsense-indicators reading max.

One touch and one more syntax-sinew cracks,
Its errors long concealed by speech-routine
But now laid bare by methods quick and clean,
Not premonitions of the headman's axe.

Now it's not heads that fall as usage slacks
But customs, forms of life, whatever's been
At stake and summoned you to intervene
Without the aid of thumbscrews, wheels, and racks.

Still it's a hardy subject who'll relax
As you, talk-torturing Torquemada, glean
Some choice mis-speakings fit to quarantine,
Then keep in mind as instances to tax

The next collocutor who gamely stacks
Such errors up yet flees that primal scene
And tells himself that word-and-thought hygiene
Of your late-Tolstoy kind had him make tracks.

# 53 On Whistling it Instead

*My day passes between logic, whistling, going for walks,
and being depressed. I wish to God that I were more
intelligent and everything would finally become clear to
me – or else that I needn't live much longer.*

'Might as well whistle it', Frank Ramsey said.
'Poor Ludwig – going on about how they
Who've naught that's vaguely relevant to say
Should just shut up. Else whistle it instead,

Or, if this doesn't work (take that as read!),
More sensibly decide to spend the day
In doing logic, walking, giving way
To the black dog, or whatnot. Best he shed

The fool idea that drove him to embed
All thoughts within the multiplex array
Of 'language-games' or 'forms of life' that may,
For all he knows, get tangled in his head

And leave him so disastrously misled
By just the sorts of nonsense he'd portray
Himself as clearing up. Whistling's okay
If latching onto some melodic thread

Helps get him past that old neurotic dread
That things won't hang together, thoughts might stray
From wisdom's path, or his own words betray
How close he feels the demon madness tread.

Tell Ludwig: when you first get out of bed,
Please ponder whether logic's grey-on-grey
Beats walks and whistling if you'd keep at bay
Those doubts and fears so deeply interbred.

# 54 False belief, first person

*If there were a verb meaning 'to believe falsely', it would not have any significant first-person present indicative.*

This I believe, though falsely' – it's absurd!
The Cretan Liar left us some recourse,
But note the shift: first person now, not third.

How think, when it's my own, that voice just heard,
That any listener-in might take its force?
'This I believe, though falsely' – it's absurd!

And yet, the inside view's a little blurred,
The paradox occluded there, at source.
Just note the shift: first person now, not third.

From Cretan Epimenides no word
Of false beliefs, just logic's Trojan Horse.
'This I believe, though falsely' – it's absurd!

Thought-blocks avoided are thought-blocks deferred,
A ploy your false-believer might endorse.
Just note the shift: first person now, not third.

Yet you, self-searcher, faced them undeterred,
Truth-value gaps that presaged full divorce.
'This I believe, though falsely' – it's absurd!
Just note the shift; first-person now, not third.

# 55 Philosophy and Crime Novels

*More wisdom is contained in the best crime fiction than in*
*philosophy.*

## I

I tell them, Moore and Russell: it's the 'tecs,
The hard-boiled US ones, not British cops
With truncheon, cuffs, and whistle round their necks,
Who might, if we'd just let them, come out tops

As our best guides in all the logic-checks,
The proofs-of-concept, swift deductive hops,
And brilliant guesswork certain to perplex
The plodding officer whose penny drops

Just after he, the private eye with sex-
Appeal and wit to match, at one stroke mops
The whole bad business up and loves to vex
Police Squad when their operation flops.

## II

I say: dear colleagues, slaves of academe,
Tight-bottled flies, and concept-cops: you'll not
Do better than look out for a good team
Of poachers-turned-gamekeepers trained to spot

The dodgy alibi, the fraudster's scheme,
The weasel clause, the fly-entangling plot,
The cleverest bank-job, and that favourite theme
Of good crime-thrillers: how the villain's got

His well-deserved come-uppance yet must seem,
To a fair-minded reader, just a jot
Less gifted, worldly-wise, and on-the-beam
Than seasoned 'tecs. It's they whose second-shot,

Hence all the worthier *succès d'estime*
In catching crooks can teach us quite a lot,
Us poor philosophers, in what's downstream
Of any fresh attempt to find some slot

Where fine detective-work might yet redeem
The (face it!) ever onward-creeping rot
Of intellects in hock to the regime
Of circumspect like-mindedness to blot

Such blameless copy-books. If their pipe-dream
Has thinking tie in readily with what
Last set the agenda, mine's to pick the cream
Of smart crime-writers to untie the knot.

# 56 Belief in the causal nexus is superstition . . . .

*The solution of the riddle of life in space and time lies outside space and time. (It is certainly not the solution of any problems of natural science that is required).*

*It is all one to me whether or not the typical western scientist understands or appreciates my work, since he will not in any case understand the spirit in which I write.*

I

Well, Ludwig, you've a gathering of the best
And brightest lined up ready with applause
For your idea that any talk of 'cause'
In physics can't survive the simplest test

Of scientific warrant, like the rest
Of those mere abstract quiddities like 'laws
Of nature', 'forces', and whatever draws
The charge that Newton famously addressed

To quaint scholastic types who'd still invest
Their faith in what the well-trained mind abhors:
That old proclivity to clutch at straws
And conjure suchlike phantoms in their quest

For speculative insights that transgressed
The ground-rules of experiment so flaws
In theory went without the needful pause
When observation made them manifest.

II

'Hypotheses non fingo', Newton wrote,
And Locke before him, both intent to chase
All talk of causes out and so embrace,
Like you, a science anxious to devote

Itself to keeping science well afloat
In turbulent times but also, just in case
This sparked controversy, to set its face
Against all notions that might rock the boat,

Such as – here shades of Galileo, note! –
The kind of explanation that would base
Itself on causal powers, or choose to place
Excessive faith in causes that demote

God's sovereign power, remove what underwrote
That tale of mortal sin redeemed by grace
Of divine intervention, and make space
For science as religion's antidote.

### III

They're still around, the sceptics who reject,
Like you, all causal talk but whose adhoc
And, frankly, unconvincing ploys to block
Its burgeoning self-evidence as checked

Against the record lead one to suspect
That they, like you, have maybe taken stock
Of just how far things have moved on since Locke
Whose sceptic views in this regard reflect

Such gaps in knowledge as would disaffect
The best-trained mind from managing to clock
Up positive results. Else these might knock
The sceptic off his perch, or bring the sect

Of nay-sayers, like you, to redirect
Their thinking, make terms quickly with the shock,
And see how such advances may so rock
Their sceptical beliefs that they elect

To seek out causes, see how things connect
At deeper levels, and no longer mock,
As you do here, the causal-realist flock
For explanations used to good effect.


IV


Yet it goes deeper, takes in issues far
Removed, you'd think, from any that arose
In prickly dealings on your part with those,
The science hegemons, who set the bar

Of group-allegiance high enough to mar
Your prospects in their bailiwick, expose
What they deemed your shortcomings, and foreclose
Whatever portals Cambridge left ajar.

But then, think how peripheral they are,
Those issues, when compared with all that goes
To make it clear just why you'd so oppose
Causation figuring in the repertoire

Of working notions reckoned on a par
With 'thought', 'mind', 'feeling', and – who knows? –
'Spirit' or 'soul', so strongly the wind blows
From each new science theme-park or bazaar.

Each instance seems to leave a psychic scar,
An unhealed wound that your self-image owes
To soul's refusal of what flesh bestows
On every god's reluctant avatar.

# 57 . . . . the liberating word . . . .

*The philosopher strives to find the liberating word, that is,*
*the word that finally permits us to grasp what up to now*
*has intangibly weighed down upon our consciousness.*
*Sometimes, in doing philosophy, one just wants to utter an*
*inarticulate sound.*

*Philosophy may in no way interfere with the actual use of*
*language; it can in the end only describe it . . . . It leaves*
*everything as it is.*

I

Always an open question: to what end
This coming hour, or day, or maybe year
Of life that, thought-entangled, I shall spend –
As always – teetering between hope and fear.

Two paths my thoughts pursue, two ways they bend,
Each with its terminus both far and near,
The further off for every false word penned,
The closer as alternatives come clear.

Those end-points have mixed messages to send,
Flat contraries, you'd think, but let them steer
Your thinking for a while and then attend:
Is it that liberating word you hear?

Or is it, just conceivably, a blend
Of inchoate vocables that greets your ear,
And any dawning sense it may portend
Mere noise that drowns the truth you hold so dear.

Call sense the outcome, noise the subtrahend
Whose taking-off has nonsense disappear;
Still it's short-term, the help such filters lend
As untruth's lords of licence get in gear.

Yet think: how should the saving word transcend
The furthest limit of this noise-filled sphere
If not by its contriving to extend
The bounds of sense until they have it veer

So far off-course that any dividend
For your life's quest can only be the sheer
Word-weariness of all who apprehend
How it may go both ways at thought's frontier?


II

Barbarians, idiots, those who spoke no Greek!
So the Greeks thought, and so they must think, too,
For whom the inarticulate cry, or shriek,
Or sigh, or bar-bar-babbling has to do

With cultural deprivation, or some freak
Of nature, or more probably what you,
Dear Ludwig, choose to treat as an oblique
Expression of how, finally, you're through –

If just for now – with all it takes to speak,
Articulate, or ceaselessly pursue
Those senses that in one direction seek
Their liberating word-bolt from the blue,

While in the other, shorn of that mystique,
They seek such sounds as pay the tribute due
To silence, nonsense, or the stubborn streak
Of barbarism that has us review

Such transcendental options. Not so bleak,
This thought that we'd do well to treat those two
Linguistic *ne plus ultra*'s as the peak
Of that peculiar gift of yours that drew,

From suchlike voyages up aporia's creek,
This upshot: common usage may eschew
Such far-out language-games, but *Sprachkritik*,
Though 'leaving everything as it is', must hew

To all you say, or show, of the unique
Though Beckett-like resolve to question who,
Or what, might voice those cries that sometimes wreak
On kindred minds the *agenbit* you knew.

# 58 Bringing out differences

*Hegel seems to me to be always wanting to say that things that look different are really the same. Whereas my interest is in showing that things which look the same are really different. I was thinking of using as a motto for my book a quotation from 'King Lear': 'I'll show you differences'. The remark 'you'd be surprised' wouldn't be a bad motto either.*

'I'll show you differences' – I cite King Lear.
Good motto; runner up, 'you'd be surprised'.
Both apt enough if we'd but ears to hear.

Kent sets the tone: uncouth, uncivilized!
He'll have no fawning rogue mock Lear's estate.
Good motto; runner-up, 'you'd be surprised'.

Stark mad, yet hold him at no lower rate.
I stand with him, that trusty liegeman, Kent.
He'll have no fawning rogue mock Lear's estate.

Who else but he foreknew the dire event,
Lear and Cordelia dead, cosmos unhinged?
I stand with him, that trusty liegeman, Kent.

They err who'd wink at differences infringed;
Like Hegel, they'd ensure all ends the same.
Lear and Cordelia dead, cosmos unhinged!

They'd soon dead-level every language-game,
See sense undone and chaos come again.
Like Hegel, they'd ensure all ends the same.

Naught but disorder stalks that regimen!
It's Edmund's, Goneril's, and Regan's realm.
See sense undone and chaos come again.

No ordered set that they'd not overwhelm,
Those would-be rulers, monarchs of misrule:
It's Edmund's, Goneril's, and Regan's realm.

For their brave opposite, consult the Fool;
Hear nonsense turn their discourse on its head,
Those would-be rulers, monarchs of misrule.

'I'll show you differences': as soon as said,
Kent's dictum tells us 'pay the Fool due heed,
Hear nonsense turn their discourse on its head'.

'You'd be surprised', my second motto: read
The play and learn from Kent, Fool, and mad Lear,
Perhaps to your surprise, how follies plead
We watch for wisdom's coastline to come clear.

# 59 On Riddles

*The riddle does not exist.*

*For an answer which cannot be expressed the question too cannot be expressed.*

*If a question can be put at all, then it can also be answered.*

I

Bertie would say: that's fine, just tell the Sphinx!
Philosophy for him's one endless riddle
Of problems yet unsolved but set to jinx
His restless intellect and have him fiddle
With words and formulas until he thinks
'That's it, I've cracked it: now excluded middle
And other rules of logic serve as links
And proof except for those with thumbs to twiddle'.

That's why my links with him became so fraught
We almost parted company, he still
The problem-solving, Sphinx-addicted sort
Who deemed philosophy a kind of drill
For getting rid of obstacles to thought,
While I said, 'Bertie, puzzle as you will,
There's no such clearance-method to be taught
Since no technique or problem-fixer's skill

Whereby the Oedipus of Sophocles,
Or anyone thus placed, might yet contrive
To work things out, more knowingly reprise
The situation, and in time arrive
At just the answer destined to appease
A Sphinx whose riddles men must vainly strive
To solve once cautioned: 'my opaque decrees
Are those no mortal reasoner may survive'.

## II

No Oedipus, that Bertie – last one you'd
Put down as hapless victim of his fate,
More captain of it, as you might conclude
From his unflagging drive to get things straight,
Leave nothing unresolved, seek certitude
On each dilemma, every last debate
From maths and logic to a multitude
Of 'social issues', his to adjudicate.

Yet, you could tell, that passion had its price,
Left him dissatisfied, frustrated, prone
To doubts, misgivings, and the sacrifice
Of other, worthier passions to atone
For some deep failure, like a secret vice,
When paradoxes loomed, like bombshells thrown
Into the set-theoretic paradise
That he, Hilbert and Cantor made their own.

# III

I owed him much; not just for getting my
*Tractatus* into print and finding ways
To stop those Cambridge fellows fighting shy
Of 'that queer German', but for all the days
Back then – no more, alas! – when he and I
Would talk about that book of mine and raise
Deep issues that, long after, I'd still try
To recollect from his deft turns of phrase.

But always, listening to him, I could hear
That nervous strain behind the outward show
Of intellectual power, a constant fear
That other claims to fame of his might go
The way of 'Russell's barber', or the sheer
Blank terror that assailed him when some *faux
Pas* in his reasoning process might appear,
To him at least, a mental body-blow.

I often thought to say: 'dear Russell, what
Compulsion is it drives that ceaseless need
To find solutions where the problem's not –
And cannot be – expressed in terms agreed
Upon and plain enough to show you've got
The sought-for answer there if you'd just heed
Its formulation – else you're talking rot,
Or don't have logic-skills quite up to speed'.

158

# IV

You're much too kind to say so (to my face),
But it's long been apparent – to a few
Close friends of ours, so not another case
Of my famed paranoia – that you grew
More distant from me, seemed intent to space
Our meetings out and show the world that you
And I no longer managed to embrace,
For friendship's sake, our differences of view.

Yet, Bertie, why suppose it's some retreat,
On my part, from the rigorous standards set
By you, Moore and your 'chums' that I must meet
If I'm to 'keep my end up' and not let
'Backsliding tendencies' or – not to beat
About the bush – my scarcely hidden debt
To dubious 'continental' types defeat
Those hopes you placed on me when we first met.

No question that it's you, Oedipus Rex
Of our Thebes-on-the-Cam, who need to take
Due cognisance of how they rise to vex
Your suffering soul, those riddles for whose sake
You'd have your mental life a running hex
Of displaced psychic posers, 'make-or-break'
Short-lived 'solutions', and scarce heeded checks
On just what chronic needs are here at stake.

For, Bertie, if one lesson's to be learned
From our blest-cursed encounter, it's that none
Meet cross-roads with their choice of route discerned
Yet unprescribed and futures yet to run
Their chancy course – not plagued by guilt unearned,
So far as they can know, since all they've done
Has somehow, unaccountably returned
Upon their heads, a tale far back begun.

The myths abound – St. Ludwig ('plaster saint
Indeed!', some say), half-genius, half-mad,
'Runs in his family', or else – with faint
Though pointed Sophoclean echoes – 'had
To happen, go like that, work out the taint
Of evil laid on him by Karl, his Dad,
The Kaiser's armourer, whose harsh restraint
Crushed tenderer spirits like his own ironclad!'.

And so my strange personae take the stage
In Cambridge and beyond, while you, my erst-
While mentor, friend, and sparring-partner gauge
How best I'm to be dealt with since thus cursed
With that strange need of genius: to assuage
The restless demons ready-primed to burst,
Eyes bright or blazing, from decorum's cage
And bid you do your average best or worst.

# VI

And yet, dear Bertie, who most benefits
Humanity, or does most to allay
Its miseries: he who must try his wits
Incessantly against some latest way
To pose or solve a riddle no-one pits
Or knows how to unriddle unless they
Already, somehow, have a key that fits
And hence no crypted secret to betray? . . . .

Or: he who, Oedipal in this at least,
Comes – better late than never! – to accept
Life's mysteries and therefore to have ceased,
Unlike you, Bertie, the vain quest that kept
Us captive to that scaffolding we'd pieced
So abstractly together that they crept
Up stealthily, my doubts, until the beast
Turned unperplexing Sphinx before it leapt.

# 60 Learning, Re-arranging, Seeing Aspects

*We learn by rearranging what we know . . . .*

*We feel that even if all possible scientific questions be answered, the problems of life have still not been touched at all. Of course there is then no question left, and just this is the answer.*

I (Wittgenstein)

'We learn by rearranging what we know.'
See how the curious child lays out his toys.
Time tells what new arrangements have to show.

It's time calls time when old ones have to go,
A use-by date for all that she enjoys.
We learn by rearranging what we know.

Some chance gestalt may briefly stay the flow
But not the shake-up process it deploys:
Time tells what new arrangements have to show.

Science declares 'it's to my works you owe
Each break-through', but that's for the lab-coat boys:
We learn by rearranging what we know.

Rather, it's by the switching to-and-fro
Of aspects that we tilt their equipoise.
Time tells what new arrangements have to show.

It's how a twice-cocked ear, inclined just so,
Hears each soft note despite the background noise.
We learn by rearranging what we know.

Change switch-rates till no ghostly afterglow
Remains to haunt the aspect it alloys.
Time tells what new arrangements have to show;
We learn by rearranging what we know.


II (Scientific Realist's Response)

'See X as Y and Y is what we see.'
A simpleton's idea, I have to say.
There's how things are and how they seem to be.

This aspect-flipping makes no sense to me;
Won't let you know what X is either way!
'See X as Y and Y is what we see.'

I say it's all this duff philosophy
That's leading science-hostile types astray.
There's how things are and how they seem to be.

Just stick to Ptolemy's astronomy
And let your projects fall out as they may.
'See X as Y and Y is what we see.'

Don't have some haughty scientist decree
'X *just is* X, whatever's on display:
There's how things are and how they seem to be'.

Then you'd turn realist and ignore what he,
Your Wittgenstein, so labours to convey.
'See X as Y and Y is what we see'?
There's how things are and how they seem to be.


III (Scientific Realist, continued)

It's by the ephebes ye shall know them best.
Cathode-ray-tube or light-bulb, type unknown?
Let physics prof and ephebe make the test.

The ephebe (physics student), though impressed
By all those wires, says 'light-bulb' – cover blown!
It's by the ephebes ye shall know them best.

The prof says 'Cathode-ray-tube', gently, lest
The student says 'that's how *you* see it' (groan!).
Let physics prof and ephebe make the test.

He, Wittgenstein, would let the matter rest,
Say 'different points of view, each to his own'.
It's by the ephebes ye shall know them best

Since he'd have them ignore how we've progressed,
How knowledge grows, and how that growth is shown.
Let physics prof and ephebe make the test.

Bad case of physics-envy, I'd suggest,
Failed scientist holed up in his safety-zone.
It's by the ephebes ye shall know them best.

Not aspect Y but object X, our quest –
Its structure, workings, powers as yet unknown!
Let physics prof and ephebe make the test;
It's by the ephebes ye shall know them best.


IV (Wittgenstein)

I 'failed at science', yes, but by *its* lights,
Those dazzlers that succeed just where they fail:
Why let its noontide glare invade our nights?

I once said 'don't stay up there on the heights
Of cleverness, descend to custom's vale'.
I 'failed at science', yes, but by its lights.

For who's to say those life-transforming flights
Of science tell a life-enhancing tale?
Why let its noontide glare invade our nights?

And why assume, if said tale then invites
More doubts, that it dictates the progress-scale?
I 'failed at science', yes, but by its lights.

We 'see things as' some life-form guides our sights,
Finds them a place in its, not techne's, pale.
Why let that noontide glare invade our nights?

For nights are when vale-dwellers put to rights
Those high crimes ventured for the science-grail.
I 'failed at science', yes, but by its lights.

What, then, if they, the clueless neophytes,
Find more sustaining life-forms to unveil?
Why let that noontide glare invade our nights?
I 'failed at science', yes, but by its lights.

# 61 Trees, tragedy, breaking-points

*You get tragedy when the tree, instead of bending, breaks.*

*If in life we are surrounded by death, then in the health of our intellect we are surrounded by madness.*

I

Not mine, the kind of life to break that tree;
More one to have it twist, bend, grow awry.
Dante's, the genre: tragi-comedy.

The 'tragic' label's mere hyperbole,
What critics choose when they've some kite to fly:
Not mine, the kind of life to break that tree.

Yes, they've found life-events that seemed a key
To thought-events, or hook to hang them by.
Dante's, the genre: tragi-comedy.

For it's no Lear or Hamlet whom you see,
And feel 'there but by Grace of God go I'.
Not mine, the kind of life to break that tree.

No 'smack of Hamlet' in me – by Act Three
He's talking wildly, fit to certify!
Dante's, the genre: tragi-comedy.

I grant you, Lear's a better fit for me,
Though frankly one whose size I'm loth to try:
Not mine, the kind of life to break that tree.

Then there's my master Tolstoy who'd decree
That pitfalls wait on tragic falls-from-high.
Dante's, the genre: tragi-comedy.

Mine the mixed mode where each peripety
Gives Lear-like destined denouements the lie.
Not mine, the kind of life to break that tree.

O, I've had sufferings enough, but we
Mind-dwellers crave no Act V time to die.
Dante's, the genre: tragi-comedy.
Not mine, the kind of life to break that tree.


## II


Close-tangled boughs, like thoughts, are apt to bend;
Trunk-breakage odds are shortened as they're shed.
No thought but has some added strength to lend.

It's why our lives enjoy a dividend
At each new sticking-point to which they're led:
Close-tangled boughs, like thoughts, are apt to bend

Or flex, not break. The many hours I'd spend
In mental toil found rotten fruit to shred.
No thought but has some added strength to lend.

They bring no tragic glories at life's end
Yet, tree-instructed, show what can't be said:
Close-tangled boughs, like thoughts, are apt to bend.

Let thought not foster cravings to transcend
Its earthly ligaments but show instead
No thought but has some added strength to lend.

I show it plainly, if they'd just attend:
By lying low we may just inch ahead.
Close-tangled boughs, like thoughts, are apt to bend.

In tragedy, when dire events impend,
We view the 'promised end' with fear and dread.
No thought but has some added strength to lend,

Since thinking, unlike tragedy, can fend
Off every stroke that takes its death as read.
Close-tangled boughs, like thoughts, are apt to bend.

Let's just say that from time to time I've penned
Some *pensées* fit for thinking's daily bread.
No thought but has some added strength to lend;
Close-tangled boughs, like thoughts, are apt to bend

III

In lives, thoughts, trees some fractures may occur,
Some mental gales leave chaos in their wake,
Freak gusts disturb the gentlest woodland stir.

Thoughts buckle, storms assail the Douglas Fir,
And life-lines twist to meet the course they take.
In lives, thoughts, trees some fractures may occur.

It's when old habits order 'as you were!'
That mind-storms do most damage, branches break,
Freak gusts disturb the gentlest woodland stir.

They'll say, and truly, 'nothing serves to spur
New thoughts like having old foundations shake'.
In lives, thoughts, trees some fractures may occur.

Yet, break-point reached, all concepts fade and blur
As reason yields its tempest-quelling stake.
Freak gusts disturb the gentlest woodland stir.

No thinker but must reckon it a slur
When told they've gone full-Lear for wisdom's sake.
In lives, thoughts, trees some fractures may occur

Yet not for those, like me, whose minds confer
The durance to equilibrate each quake.
Freak gusts disturb the gentlest woodland stir.

Suits psycho-sleuth and crack-up connoisseur,
That stuff for vulgar Freudians to half-bake.
In lives, thoughts, trees some fractures may occur

And feed such tastes but my poor ephebes err
If that's the sense they'd have my life's work make.
Freak gusts disturb the gentlest woodland stir;
In lives, thoughts, trees some fractures may occur.

# 62 A wonderful life . . . .

*'Tell them I've had a wonderful life . . . .'*

## I

So many ways those last words might be meant!
Let's try: sincere, face-value, meant as said.
How else construe a dying man's intent?

And yet, we've read you, read about you, spent
Long hours, years, lives absorbing all we've read.
How many ways those last words might be meant.

Small sign you gave of some ironic bent
That should have told us straight: we'd been misled.
How else construe a dying man's intent?

A serious man, not apt to circumvent
The truth, or seek to have false witness spread.
How many ways those last words might be meant!

We must believe you, else your life's work went
For naught when you, naysayer, struck it dead.
How else construe a dying man's intent?

We trusters say: let us reorient
Our thinking, not break faith at your deathbed.
How many ways those last words might be meant!

Yet let's not duck the challenge they present
To those who'd thought to live inside your head.
How now construe a dying man's intent?
How many ways those last words might be meant!

171

# II

Let's say '*vita nuova*, life renewed,
Transfigured instantly in retrospect'.
Why think life-options end as lives conclude?

More than a change of outlook, mind or mood,
Those words make good your 'seeing-as' effect.
Let's think vita *nuova*, life renewed.

Life-aspects from death's door thus briefly viewed
May leave no scene unaltered since last checked:
Why think life-options end as lives conclude?

Blithe spirits counsel 'change of attitude'
But no such soul-malaise can touch their sect.
Let's think *vita nuova*, life renewed.

On wanhope's egg you melancholics brood
Till, long tight-sealed, it's revelation-pecked.
Why think life-options end as lives conclude?

This reading has your tortured life imbued
With hopes redeemed from hopes mislaid or wrecked:
Let's think *vita nuova*, life renewed.

Else how might any life as dark-side skewed
As yours catch sight of joys they'd once neglect?
Why think life-options end as lives conclude?
Let's think *vita nuova*, life renewed.

# III

Maybe we'd best account you satirist,
Self-disabused of hope's deceptive gleam.
What's then to save of each last chance you missed?

The last we hear of, just before your tryst
With Tolstoy's God, was every saint's stock theme.
Maybe we'd best account you satirist.

Your gift to those who seek yet further grist
To their harsh mill, this pietistic seam:
What's then to save of each last chance you missed?

No cynic who'd apply the devil's twist
To dying words but buys this handy scheme:
Maybe we'd best account you satirist.

Then it's your life's-work pivots on the gist
Of words fit to perplex the Seraphim.
What's then to save of each last chance you missed?

Call in some sense-inverting casuist
And they'll have you take one for satire's team.
Maybe we'd best account you satirist

And hide our scorn when those recidivist
Truth-sticklers next revive their old regime.
What's then to save of each last chance you missed?
Maybe we'd best account you satirist.

# IV

'Tell them', you said, but who knows what's to tell,
What change of heart those seven last words may bear?
How conjure paradise from psychic hell?

The ambiguous rumour of a passing bell
Is how they fall on ears caught unaware.
'Tell them', you said, but who knows what's to tell?

That ambiguity exerts its spell,
Fills some with cautious hope, some with despair:
How conjure paradise from psychic hell?

Some say the known facts of your life compel
An earthbound gloss not offered up as prayer.
'Tell them', you said, but who knows what to tell?

'Spent all his life as if in a monk's cell',
They say; 'why think the torment ended there,
By conjuring paradise from psychic hell?'.

'Why claim to know what soul-event befell',
Some counter, 'beyond what those plain words declare?'
'Tell them', you said, but who knows what to tell?

What if your manic paths ran parallel,
The moment's bliss, the *saison en enfer*,
The conjured paradise, the psychic hell?
'Tell them', you said, but who knows what to tell?

www.ingramcontent.com/pod-product-compliance
Lightning Source LLC
Chambersburg PA
CBHW071915160426
42812CB00097B/1074